FATHER, I NEVER KNEW YOU

FATHER, I NEVER KNEW YOU

Power of Forgiveness

DR. NORMAN E. HUTCHINS

Noahs Ark Publishing Service
Beverly Hills, California

Father, I Never Knew You: Power of Forgiveness

ISBN 979-8-9920102-0-6

Published by:

Noahs Ark Publishing Service
8549 Wilshire Blvd., Suite 1442
Beverly Hills, CA 90211
www.noahsarkpublishing.com

Creative Concept & Development by Laval W. Belle
Edited by Carolyn Billups
Graphic Design by Christopher C. White
Interior Design by Andrea Reider

To the loving memory of my mother
Doris Hopper Hutchins.

To all of the young boys and girls who went
through life without a biological father.

TABLE OF CONTENTS

FOREWORD

Lest we blame the people and not the realities that have motivated their mass exodus, it is necessary to understand why people choose not to attend church. One primary reason people attempt to justify their departure is the church's lack of authenticity and forgiveness. These deficiencies have left many feeling alienated and disillusioned in a world yearning for connection and grace.

The Black church has historically been the heart and soul of the Black community; it was the rallying point and place for Black people and Black issues. It has long been the leading institution supporting Black justice, business, education, children and youth, family, and overall progression. The Black church was and remains the nexus of Black success, providing a foundation of hope and strength. It has always been essential to be part of this institution, the one space to which children leaving their communities of origin were expected to pledge allegiance, no matter where they moved. How, then, could such a heinous and egregious event as rejection or shame happen to any child reared in this environment?

In this compelling and deeply personal book, Dr. Norman Hutchins reveals the dark side of what was meant to be a safe space. Through the forensics of his life experiences—marked by rejection and shame—he masterfully uncovers the challenges and opportunities for 21st-century Christianity. His story is a testimony of resilience and a call to action for churches to return to authenticity, forgiveness, and grace.

This book is not merely a read; it is a tool for revival in the church and a call to rebuild the church's sacred role as a source of empowerment, unity, and hope. I uncompromisingly recommend this book to every believer and kingdom builder. Let it not just rest on your bookshelf but take root in your heart and actions. Hats off to Dr. Norman Hutchins—God has done it again!

Bishop Liston Page II

CHAPTER ONE

PREACHING TO THE CHICKENS

It was about 1969. I remember because I was just turning eight years old when my mother separated from the man I thought was my father. Later in life I would learn that he was not. He was an alcoholic who was verbally and physically abusive to my mother.

My mom was the breadwinner of the family. I don't know what he did. I don't like repeating his name, but for the sake of this story, his name was James. All he used to do was ride a bicycle around town. He was the kind of old man that everybody knew. I never really had conversation with him because, if I saw him sober at the house, I was afraid. If I saw him drunk, I ran. He never had a lot of words for me either, as I'm sure he knew I wasn't his. My mama got pregnant with me while he was in jail during one of his episodes. One of his ways of punishing me, which was truly overkill, was abuse.

When I was about six or seven years old, my friends and I were outside playing one day. I had a Big Wheel; a big plastic toy tricycle with three wheels and an adjustable seat. It was really nice. We were standing around just talking and I cussed, not realizing James was riding close by on his bicycle. He overheard me, stopped and yelled, *"Norman!"* Man, I was so scared! Right then I knew he heard me. Then he doubled down and shouted, *"Follow me."* Now here I am, on a little Big Wheel tricycle and he's telling me to follow him! This man started riding all around town. I remember passing by the park, the community swimming pool the Simon Bright apartments and by this time I'm crying. I mean I can't go any farther! He was on a bike and knew exactly what he was doing. This was his way of punishing me. Every time I would stop, he'd shout, *"Come on, keep going, follow me!"* He even made me fall down. From that point on, I just cried and cried and cried. Even in my little mind I knew he was wrong. He didn't hit or lay his hands on me, but I tell you what, I called what he did calculated private abuse. Anytime he walked through the door I knew my one and only obligation was to stay out of his way. I would go hide a lot of times and play under the house. If he ever called my name, I knew I was in trouble. He always blamed me for everything. Anytime he was upset with my mother, he was upset with me. Anytime he abused my mom, he abused me. He would make up stuff.

One evening my mother had taken all she could. An argument had ensued and they were fussing and fighting. Of course, he was probably drunk because he was always drunk. He went to grab his .22 caliber rifle and came after my mother pointing it right at her. Immediately she grabbed the kids, and my two older brothers, Michael and Jimmy, came running! They tackled him to the ground and grabbed his gun. By this time my mom, a couple of my sisters and I went running up the street to my grandma's house who lived close to two blocks away. Now, back then, something you didn't do in the South was call the police during a domestic dispute. If the police came to your house, they either beat or arrested everybody.

Even though my mother was being abused she still loved James, and certainly didn't want him going to jail. He'd already been in and out of jail for whatever reason. If my memory serves me correctly, he probably went into his room after the incident and fell asleep because he was so drunk.

Goodbye North Carolina, Hello Delaware

Eight of the twelve of us lived at home. The very next day we all got in the car to escape the drama and dysfunction. That is, all of us who could comfortably fit in that big old Model-T Ford. It was an old car with a hump in the back that I sat on for the seven-hour ride to Millsboro, Delaware from Kingston, North Carolina. That Model-T Ford was like a big, four door limousine. It had grey interior and a great big round steering wheel. You had to manually crank the windows open and shut. The front windshield was huge with long windshield wipers. I used to love sitting behind the wheel when the car was parked in the yard and pretend I was driving. Whoever couldn't fit in the Model-T rode the Greyhound bus to our new home in Delaware where my mother's mother and dad, my grandmom and granddad, lived. I don't know what happened to James after that.

The first time I had ever seen an indoor bathroom with water flowing from an inside faucet was in Millsboro. It was also the first time I experienced going to school with White children and having a White teacher, which was a real shock! I experienced a change in my family and my world at the same time.

My granddaddy, Clifton Phillips, was a sharecropper. The property's landowner let him live in a house on his property that also had chicken houses on it. As part of the arrangement, he got to stay in the house.In exchange, he had to take care of the chickens, which was pretty much a 24/7 job. His pay for all that work included living rent-free, plus whatever granddaddy earned for managing the chickens.

We called it a chicken house because there were thousands and thousands of chickens living inside. Every day my grandfather would have to feed these chickens and collect their eggs, because they were laying hens. You could see them by the thousands in their small chicken coops.

During the summer I helped my grandfather collect the eggs. We pushed a carriage that ran through the center of all the houses. Once a particular room was entered, eggs were collected from the different coops. After collecting the eggs, we sent them to hatchery companies to create more laying hens. Many times, the eggs were also sold in markets and sometimes, when the hens grew really big, they were sold in grocery stores.

Helping my grandfather collect eggs and feed the chickens became a normal thing for me. Of course, he never paid me, but what he did was pay us with Rice Krispies cereal and vanilla pudding. *Ohhh,* he used to make some good vanilla pudding!

I've Always Loved Church

Our family joined Holy Trinity Church of God in Christ in Millsboro, Delaware. From my beginnings when I was much smaller, I've always loved church. Some of my younger sisters and brothers and I would play church and, of course, I had to be the preacher. So, I would preach, and we all would sing and praise the Lord! Holy Trinity was a powerful Pentecostal church and I loved hearing the pastor, Elder Goldsberry, preach. He is deceased now. After listening to him preach, I would go back home and while in the chicken house, would stop and preach that same message to the chickens! I would tell them, *"You gotta be saved! You need to give your life to God!"* I mean Billy Graham didn't have nothing on me because at eight years old I had about 50,000 members in my congregation! Word started getting around about my preaching to these chickens, and sometimes people would sneak around just to see if they could hear me preaching to them.

I remember there were several roosters in each chicken coop. This was important because they helped their hens lay eggs. At the time, I didn't understand how that worked, but we know now. Anyway, the roosters were very territorial. If they saw me taking the eggs or if I even looked like I was approaching the hens, the back of their necks would stand up, like they were in a fighting position. I wasn't afraid of them because I saw what happened when folks would start acting up in church. I guess they must have been casting out demons, so I did the same thing. I would say, *"Roosters, the Lord rebuke you! I cast you out devil! Get out!"* That rooster would fuss and fuss and if he tried to come toward me, I'd pick up the trough and hit him in the head! He would dance around like he was drunk, and of course he left me alone. That reminded me of what people did in church. You know, how they would get full of the spirit and dance around like they were drunk and then finally fall out. So, I figured if I hit him in the head he would dance around and fall out under the spirit.

It's interesting though, I didn't realize it as a child but thought about it years ago as an adult. Chicken coop preaching became a safe place for me. Not only did I preach to the chickens, but I also told them everything I was dealing with and going through. The thing about these chickens is, they never disagreed. They always said the same thing and to me it was, *"Yes!"* When I told them to get saved, to me their answer was, *"Yes."* I developed such an attachment to them that I could walk through the house, and you know what? They treated me like I was their pastor because they didn't run from me anymore, and they didn't fight me when I took their eggs. I guess the eggs were their offering.

Now here is something interesting. When the chickens grew older, trucks came to collect them and take them to the chicken plants. There they were killed, and their parts were separated and packaged so they could be shipped off to grocery stores. When I felt like their time was drawing near for their final departure, they started looking sad to me. So, I would start preaching to them like they were getting ready to experience chicken heaven, goodness! I used to conduct a lot of funerals, because sometimes when I entered the chicken house, the chickens would be dead. I've always wondered how did they die? What was it? Why did things die?

I remember going through that chicken house, thinking of all the things I lost in my life as a small child and all the things I didn't get a chance to experience. I wasn't popular in school and had difficulty learning, but I had a wild imagination! Oh, my God, could I ever daydream!

The unique thing about my grandfather, Clifton Phillips, was he always hummed. I used to love hearing him hum. Hearing his melodic *"dodo, dooo, dodo dooo's"* did something good to my soul. I don't know how old he was when I was eight, but he was definitely old and could really get around. I watched him. I didn't have a dad, so I started picking up a lot of his traits. It was easy for him to hear me preaching to the chickens. He never told me to stop, he never did. I believe my grandfather knew I would be a preacher one day. As a matter of fact, my grandfather began telling me Bible stories. The first Bible story I remember my grandfather sharing with me was Jonah in the belly of the whale. I was having a hard time trying to figure out how in the world could a whale swallow a whole man. Oh man, but when he finished telling me the story, in my own innocent childish way, I could see the power and the miracle of God. I didn't realize it then, but I believe he was my Joshua. A lot of the things I've learned about God, even before my mother started giving me my messages, came from my grandfather after it was confirmed and prophesied, I would be a preacher.

Sometimes when I would ride to town with him, (Lord, was I afraid of his driving!), he would be humming, singing and talking about God. We would just listen as he ministered, but it was also a really sad moment too. When those trucks came to get the chickens, even though they all looked alike, it seemed like I recognized each one. For some reason, it was the way they sounded and the way they moved. I didn't realize how intelligent chickens really are. Actually, I believe some of them understood what I said. It got to a point when I came in the chicken house, they kind of greeted me. You know, it was like people waiting to find out, *"What you got for me today pastor?"* or *"What's the weather today?"* You know? I was serious! I wasn't playing games. When I came up in that chicken house, I was ready. If the preacher said, *"Y'all need to be filled with the Holy Ghost,"* I would tell the chickens, *"You need to be filled with the Holy Ghost,"* and all of them started speaking in tongues.

The chicken house was my safe place. I know it now as an adult. Children will find a place where they feel safe. Where the thoughts in their minds can purr and sometimes, they daydream to hide the pain of things they've had to endure. So, being in this chicken house alone with my grandfather was where he showed me love and taught me Bible stories. He became that pillar I needed as a young boy growing up.

Granddad was in a lot of car accidents and, to this day, I don't know how he survived so many of them. Once, he had a head-on collision that sent us running down the street because of the terribly loud sound it made. After that experience, my grandma wouldn't allow him to drive any longer, so he started walking everywhere. My grandma always warned him that he'd better stop walking outside because somebody was going to come around and hit him. She warned him over and over again for years until one day we got a phone call that granddad was hit beside the road. That's exactly how he died. I loved my granddaddy. He was my first example of a real man, and he gave me some of my first sermons. I loved the way he told me Bible stories. Like the one about Jonah in the belly of the whale. Oh my God, how he made it come alive was everything! I thank God for the Sharecropper.

Not only did I preach to the chickens, I sang to the chickens as well. You see, my mother was a piano player and a singer. She was always in charge of the choirs at Holy Trinity COGIC. I remember my mother singing, sounding like Shirley Caesar. She used to write songs as well, but never recorded any of them. Out of all the songs my mother wrote, I do remember one of them. I would be at the rehearsals, sitting right beside her at the piano. That's how I started learning to play, by watching my mother play. When I went back to the chicken house, I would turn over a chicken coop and stand up there as their choir director. Oh boy, did I have a big choir. The chickens were my choir members. I would make up songs and teach them to the chickens. Then I would preach!

When I think back on it, some of the things I was preaching were some deep-rooted secrets, pain, and hurt that I was experiencing and going through, because I had nobody to talk to. Mama was so busy trying to take care of the children. We had twelve kids on my momma's side, and I was the baby boy. She was busy working as a single mom so, that meant she was always gone. She was either working or she was at the church, and I would be there with her as much as I could.

One day my mother came home and said, *"It was prophesied through one of the older mothers in the church that God was going to make you a preacher."* I was excited because, hey I was already preaching. Anytime anybody asked me at school, *"What do you want to be?"* I always told them, *"I wanna be a preacher, I wanna be a preacher!"* Oh, and I didn't just say preacher, I wanted to be a pastor too! So, when I heard that news, *ohh* that was really exciting!

There was a youth department at our church called YPWW, which stands for Young Peoples Willing Workers. All of the young kids had to participate in different youth events and functions. Quite frequently, YPWW would host a Platform Service, and I loved them. Each child was given approximately three to five minutes to teach a lesson or preach if you could. The topic could be about Jesus on the Cross, Lazarus in the grave, the crossing of the Red Sea or Abraham and Isaac. Seemingly, I was always last and when I got up, as they say, I went for it! I could see everyone looking at me like, *"Oh wait a minute, wow! He's actually anointed!"* My pastor recognized it, my mom recognized it, as did the lady who prophesied, and all the adults. That's when they told my mom, *"You've got to work with him. You've got to teach him; you have to train him because he has been called. He is anointed to preach!"* My mother started doing just that and my pastor did too. The next thing I knew, by the time I was twelve years old, my pastor licensed me as a minister in the church.

I wasn't preaching to the chickens much anymore but every once in a while, I would help my grandfather out. Now these sermons I had preached to the chickens, I was now preaching them to real people. Wow! I was prepared in the chicken house to preach to real people!

There were also deeper things going on with me in the chicken house. I ran away from a lot of things based on an element of racism. As a young kid I really didn't understand racism. For many young Black kids, living under the umbrella of racism was just a way of life. You just thought White people were superior to and better than you. Not to mention, they lived on their side of town, and Blacks lived on their side of town. Very seldom did I run into a White person because our schools were segregated. By the time we moved to Delaware, the state was already desegregated. This was my first time going to school with White kids.

There is a chain of stores called Piggly Wiggly throughout the South. They aren't quite full-on grocery stores or supermarkets, but more like corner stores owned by White people. Many times, Robert Earl Lee and I would visit Piggly Wiggly to buy penny candy. From the time we walked into the store until we left, we were watched like a hawk. They didn't want us in there too long. The store clerks used the "N" word frequently with us, I mean it was unbelievable.

As a matter of fact, even my birth certificate had the "N" word written on it. I discovered this when it was lost, and we had to go downtown to purchase another one. When the clerk pulled it from the file and brought it to me, I saw my ethnicity was recorded as the "N" word. God knows I wish I had taken a picture of it. It was changed in that moment to reflect I was born African American.

The chicken house was a place I could go and cry when I felt sad and disappointed when life wasn't treating me fairly. I was never judged there. Everything was always the same. At the end of every year, when companies came to harvest the chickens, for me it was like a funeral or taking my best friends away from me. Then, of course, a whole new flock (we called them biddies) were delivered and they grew to become adult chickens. It was like starting all over again.

I Couldn't Read or Write

Preaching to the chickens is more than the act itself, but what it represented. It was my safe haven. I would always run to the chicken house because of problems I faced in school. It was difficult for me to learn when I was in 1st through 5th grades. I couldn't read and nobody took the time to teach me. My mom was too busy, and my grandfather couldn't read.

I was always teased in school, but I had a good plan to make them stop. I became the class clown so the kids would laugh with me and not at me. I felt it was better for me to make them laugh than for them to laugh at me.

I could never understand how at the early ages of eight, nine, ten and eleven years old, I could not read, and yet I made it through school. I don't understand it even to this day, but I'll tell you what I remember. I remember my safety zone and my safe haven, the chickens! Here's what I would do. When the teacher would say, *"Okay class, I want y'all to read this story and then I want you to write your own story then, read your story in front of the class."* I dreaded it. So, what I would do was sit there and look at the pages. I couldn't read a word. I couldn't even read my own name. By this time, I'm in the 3rd, 4th, and 5th grades. My daydreaming in the chicken house had me thinking about the stories on television while I'm collecting the eggs. Remember, I told you I was a great daydreamer. Back then there were shows like *Gilligan's Island, Bewitched, I Dream of Jeannie* and *The Partridge Family.* I remembered all of those episodes and would be in the chicken house acting out those things to the chickens too. I mean I did so much with them.

Now what I did was just scratch on my paper because I couldn't write either. I'd just scratch circles on every line. Then when it was my time to go up to read, I would stand up there in front of the class, holding that piece of paper with all the circles on it and look at my classmates. I would tell them a story from *I Dream of Jeannie* or *Gilligan's Island,* but I changed all of the names. My classmates were so excited because I would put drama in it and act out all of the different characters. I gave them their own personalities, and I mean I went for it. The kids would be laughing and clapping. By the time I finished, they gave me a standing ovation because they felt I was the best storyteller! I'll never forget it.

The teacher gave us another assignment and all of us had to be quiet. She called me over to her desk and said, *"Norman, pull up a chair and sit here."* I sat beside her, and she took my paper because we had to turn our stories in to her after we finished. She looked at all the scribbles and all she said to me was, *"I want you to read this to me again,"* and let me tell you what. I started from the top just like I did with the kids, and I read the story to her. I gave her all the same drama I gave the kids and everything. She had me whisper it to her and I did, I sure did! When I finished, she said, *"Okay, you can go back to your seat,"* and you know, she never said anything else, not that I remember. She never said, *"This is not writing,"* or asked *"Do you know how to read?"* Nothing! Of course, she wasn't my color and back then we had difficulties when it came to desegregation of schools. So, a lot of times they just kind of pushed you right through, but I didn't realize it at the time.

I didn't know how to read all the way to probably the 7th grade. Because I couldn't read or comprehend, the school staff thought I had suffered emotional damage or whatever else they may have considered to be my issue. There was a class for socially and emotionally maladjusted students. The abbreviated name of the class was Special Education, and there were only about four or five of us in it from the 7th grade. We were the laughingstock of the school. It was hard to learn because the kids in that class were considered to be the "bad kids." It was hard for the teacher because he was always dealing with problems.

I used to hate it when we went on field trips because we always rode in the little, short bus. The other classes had two or three regular size buses. When the other students saw us on that little, short bus, my God, I can almost feel the embarrassment from the experience right now.

I had nobody to teach me all the way up through the 12th grade and believe I was pushed right on through. Interestingly enough, back in that chicken coop and back at the church, when it was prophesied that I was going to be a preacher, apparently God in His own way had to teach me. How could I be a preacher if I couldn't read or study the Bible? He wanted me to go to theological seminary and so what God did was, I remember like it happened yesterday, He gave me the gift of memorization. From that point on, when I saw a word, I heard it repeated and memorized it. I started to build such a large vocabulary of words and learned to put sentences together. Then I was able to start making up sentences and began reading more. I got better and better and better! So much so I began to read and understand what vowels, nouns and adjectives were. Things got better and, I guess you could say, I became a fluent reader probably in my mid-twenties. I went to Bible college, graduated with my master's in Biblical Counseling and my Doctorate in Church Administration. The only reason I know I did not give up is because I had that safe place. Yep, yep, yep! To God be the glory. Yeah, the Safe Place.

From Special Ed to Hall of Fame

As I think about it, a lot of the dreams I've had in life, and in the chicken house preaching to the chickens, never crossed my mind as becoming reality. I graduated from Sussex Central High School in 1980 from the 12th grade as a Special Ed student. The Lord Himself taught me how to read by giving me the gift of memorization. I was able to go to Bible college and graduate with two degrees. What baffles my mind is, earlier this year in 2024 my wife and I got a call from my high school in Georgetown, Delaware. They said, *"You have been nominated and selected to be inducted to the Sussex Central High School Hall of Fame."* I was like, *"Whoa, wait a minute, somebody's playing a prank on me,"* but when I got the official letter, I couldn't believe it! From Special Ed to the Hall of Fame? From the same high school where I was teased and people laughed at me because I didn't dress properly? My mom was poor, we were all poor and now I'm being inducted into the Hall of Fame. Hmm, I need to go back and ask those chickens, *"When did we see that coming?"*

I will never forget when my wife and I attended the ceremony. The student body was there, and many people who remembered me from high school were sitting on the stage. When my name was called, I had fifteen minutes to respond, you know, to give a word of encouragement to the students. The title of my speech was *From Special Ed to Hall of Fame.* It was powerful! I shared with them some of the things I experienced during that time, like me wanting to play basketball. Well, I was the second shortest boy throughout my entire high school experience. Only one other boy was shorter than me.

So, I tried out for football and remember the coach saying to me, *"What position you want to play?"* I said, *"I want to be the quarterback."* He said, *"We got one."* I said, *"How about the tight end?"* He replied, *"We got one."* I gave him another alternative, *"How about you know, running back?"* Again, he said, *"We got that."* I said, *"Well, what positions do you have available?"* In front of all those young guys he said to me, *"We need a football!"* Man, that thing crushed me, and I'll never forget it! When I tried out for basketball, because I was the shortest guy, I didn't make it. I guess the coach took great pity on me. Because he knew I loved football and basketball, he let me join the JV team. Interestingly enough, I never played a game. I think I must have been about thirteen or fourteen years old, maybe somewhere up in there. I was the happiest guy in the world because I got to wear the uniform. You know, in the chicken house I daydreamed I was the star of the football and basketball teams! I pretended the chickens were the crowd cheering me on. I'm telling you, I used to play football with the chickens. I would run and they would move out of the way. You had to see it to understand.

I never played the game as a basketball player, but what made me happy was when we came out of the locker room, we entered the court by height. Because I was the shortest one, that meant I was always first. And the first person to get the basketball was me! That was my only job. In front of all the people waiting in the gymnasium, we dribbled all the way around the whole court. The whole team is following me as I dribbled around the court and the crowd cheered and cheered. We reach the net and I reach up like I'm getting ready to make a layup but it wasn't my job. My job was to hit the ball on the back of the backboard so the next person behind me could hit it, then the following person, and the following person, until the last person made the layup. That was the highlight of my life! I did play one game, which was actually almost the last game of the season. I think we were losing by 50 or 60 points with less than two minutes left in the game. The coach said to me, *"Norman, come on."* The people cheered for me because they knew I had never played a game. That was my moment! When I entered the game, they threw me the ball, and you know how everybody keeps saying, *"Pass it to me, pass it to me?"* Well, I'm thinking to myself, *"I ain't played the whole season and you're asking? No, no, no, no, I'm gonna go make this point!"* I was dribbling in my mind and could just see myself the same way I was in the chicken house, going up for my layup right there in that gym. When I went up for that layup, I don't know where this guy came from, he slapped that ball way up in the top bleachers and everybody just laughed and laughed and laughed and laughed. Oh my God, can you imagine being in school, everybody is there and that happens? Then you've gotta go to school the next day! Oh my God!

Well, one day I was walking through school and upstairs to an area I hadn't visited before. I thought I knew the whole school. I started hearing a sound, and the closer I got I began to recognize it. It was the school chorus. I looked in the window and listened to them singing. Right then I knew I had found my niche. When I looked in the window, I saw students, but I saw chickens too! I did that in the chicken house! I met with the teacher and told her I wanted to be in the choir. I was accepted and, boy I tell you, singing in the choir was truly my niche! Yeah! I sang in the choir, then I began to write and teach songs.

I'm sixty-one years old now and what I'm feeling right now isn't pain. I think its gratitude, that's what I think it is. It's great I got through all thatI went through. I was around family, but didn't feel like I really had family. I was kind of by myself on the streets, me and my little neighborhood. I don't know their names, but they were my best friends: LeeLee, GG, Robert Earl, who else, Chico, Donnie, who was my nephew, and me. We were like, what's the group that used to be on TV all the time? Not *The Chipmunks* but *The Little Rascals*! That's it! We were like *The Little Rascals*! We were young, grown men. I'm talking, all of us were like five, six, seven, eight years old and were this little group all over town. I remember those guys. I just don't know where they are now, but I thank God He allowed me to survive all of this.

Despise not small beginnings! It is so interesting how chickens have been such a large part of my life, but I still eat them! *Ohhh,* do I love me some good old fried chicken!

CHAPTER TWO

WHO AM I?

When I think about the title of this chapter it makes me chuckle. The first thought that comes to my mind is me growing up down in the deep south of North Carolina back in the 1960s. I can't tell you how many times I used to look at myself in the mirror as I was growing up and ask myself that very same question. *"Who am I?"* I would stare at my eyes in the mirror and wait for a response. But you know, growing up we always found our identity in our idols and the people we admired. I grew up in a community of limitations economically, socially, and physically, having to wear hand me down clothes. I really had very low self-esteem about who I was and very seldom would anybody come and speak positively into my life. Especially back in those days when you were called the "N" word. On top of that, you're a nobody and, on top of that, a bastard child. It feels like your identity changes every day. Sometimes your identity was wrapped around your dreams and what you wanted to become or daydreams about who you were. What's amazing is who would have ever thought that this little five-year-old boy would find his identity in his pastor and had dreams that screamed, *"I want to do that! I want to be a preacher and preach just like him!"* Or like my mom, singing and playing the piano! *"I want to be like that!"* That's how I found my identity.

I began listening to the radio, to my mentor idols, I call them—Andraé Crouch, James Cleveland and the O'Neal Twins. Unbelievable! I pretended I was them and that I could do what they did, but deep down inside never really believed the day would come that I'd actually be doing what I daydreamed! Here's an example for you, I used to go under the house and play with my rocks. I'd get a cigar box, turn it upside down and pretend it was a stage. Then I would gather some rocks and put them on top of the cigar box along with another rock and pretend it was me in front of a choir teaching and singing songs I had written. Then I would go get some egg cartoons and fill them up with rocks. All twelve slots! This was me imagining people on the bus. I pushed them in front of my imaginary stage, got a box, turned it upside down and turned all the other rocks outward so I'd have a big old crowd. Oh, I could daydream for hours about me teaching and singing songs and being around the world.

Finding My Identity

Looking through the telescope of time, in 1991 I was Executive Minister of Music at West Angeles Church of God in Christ. One day two White gentlemen came to my office and said they were referred by someone. Now, by this time, I'm in the recording industry. I had recorded *Saints in Praise,* one in a series of three albums. These gentlemen went on to explain that they were looking for a song to accompany the lighting of the Olympic torch! Oh my God! Can you believe it? This was to take place at the Olympic festival held at Dodger Stadium!

So, I wrote the song and headed right over to rehearsals to work with a choir of over 1,000 voices! The church was a huge Catholic Church located on Wilshire Blvd. On presentation night, I had a multicultural choir and wore my white gloves with my patent leather shoes, looking out at thousands and thousands of people. The Dodger Stadium was packed to capacity and millions of people were watching from around the world.

Halfway through the song I had written and arranged, someone suddenly tapped me on the shoulder and said, *"What does this remind you of?"* Right there in front of all of those people my mind went all the way back to Kingston, North Carolina, deep in the South when I used to be under the house with my cigar box and my rocks. I am Norman Earl Hutchins, born September 27, 1962, to Doris Hutchins, one of twelve children. I didn't know my dreams would come to me later in life. I found my identity in people I saw as I grew up.

Musically, Andraé Crouch was my musical idol. I knew and loved his music. Not in the sense as a God, but someone who really, really motivated, inspired and encouraged me. As I began to grow in age, I mimicked his music and did my best to sound like him, with his husky, raspy voice. Who would have ever thought the day would come when I would actually be sitting at the piano with Andraé Crouch, in his living room, looking at the top of his piano filled with Grammy Awards, Gold and Platinum albums and NAACP awards all around me.

I met Andraé Crouch when I was singing at a church in Banning, California. On my way to my seat, someone tapped me on the shoulder and said, *"Give me a call."* I looked up and it was Andraé Crouch. I couldn't believe it! I met him, his father and family. He invited me to sing and preach at his church where I also conducted a two-week revival, and Andre played the organ for me. So, I became the young kid of the family. The same young boy who daydreamed about his idol. I also pastored the church for Bishop Benjamin Crouch, Andraé Crouch's dad, for five years there in Banning and had opportunities to do some traveling. It never entered my mind that the little raggedy piano my Mama had in her house, that big old upright piano where I used to hide food as a kid was part of my preparation for elevation. I hid food in that old piano because, if I didn't hide my food, someone else would surely come along and eat everything.

From "Who Am I?" to "Who Do I Want To Be?"

You could always hear me beating and banging on those old piano keys. Some of the songs God gave me are still being heard around the world. Never did it enter my mind that one day I'd earn two Grammy Awards, Gold and Platinum albums, several Stellar and Dove Award nominations, and oh, a Soul Train award! All of this started when I looked in that mirror as a kid and asked myself, *"Who am I?"* That question, *"Who am I?"* turned into *"What do I want to be?"* Once I changed the question, I began to pursue things I thought I could accomplish and saw other people doing.

So, Norman Hutchins is a Preacher, Pastor, Bishop and a father, filled with passion unsealed and a desire to overcome all of the obstacles and adversities in life. All of the things I've suffered through, the things I've gone through, even as a child, through the verbal and physical abuse from my stepdad, an alcoholic.

It all turned out to be something great, because in those private, silent moments, my mind and my imagination took me to places I have experienced. I never thought I'd sing on the Grand Ole Opry stage. Never thought I'd sing on the Shrine Auditorium stage, but I daydreamed and experienced it. Wow! So, who am I? I'm someone who loves life, loves people and will do anything I can to help anybody.

At the end of each school year, particularly in the 4th through 8th grades, the teacher would always ask, "*So, what do you want to be when you grow up?*" Every year I would always answer with, "*I want to be a preacher, and I want to be a singer.*" Sometimes teachers will try to discourage you from wanting to do things they don't believe you have the ability to achieve. Back then reading and writing was a problem for me. Certainly, coming from a poor family, many times teachers tried to steer me in a direction they felt was a better fit for me at that particular moment. But, it was stuck in my brain that I wanted to be a preacher, and I wanted to be a singer.

Why Not Me?

As I mentioned earlier, my gospel mentor was Andraé Crouch. Well, growing up in our house we couldn't listen to secular music. They called it the devil's music back then, but anytime I left the house I would listen to other music genres. My favorite, my goodness, was Michael Jackson and as a preteen I could sing all of his music. The kids in school loved to hear me sing and dance like Michael. When I started writing songs, I would take Michael's songs and write my words to his melodies. Again, I never thought the day would come when I would stand on stage with him!

The event was a tribute to Sammy Davis, Jr. at the Shrine Auditorium in Los Angeles, California in the early 90s. I was at West Angeles Church of God in Christ at the time and Stevie Wonder, a member of the church, and myself, put a choir together to back Stevie as a tribute to Mr. Davis. On the night of the event, holding onto Stevie Wonder's arm, I led him on stage to the piano. All of this is like a dream. To back up a little, I'm actually in Ebony magazine where there's a picture of me directly behind him. I still have it to this day. We were singing the song *The Truth is the Light* and at the end of the show, we did the grand finale. Everyone who was on the show came out on stage and we all sang a piece of the last song. While I was standing there, the Holy Spirit began to minister to me and said, "*Just look around."* I was in my early twenties and as I began to look around the stage, I could not believe my eyes. I saw Clint Eastwood, Brooke Shields, Bill Cosby, Mike Tyson, Magic Johnson, Goldie Hawn and Don Hines. I mean the list goes on and on, but between the crowd, right at the front, about four people away from them, I saw this guy wearing black pants, a red shirt and a gold and silver chain. It was Michael Jackson, my childhood mentor! Here I am, the boy from the country, whose teachers said wouldn't be anything. I could not believe it was Michael Jackson and in that moment, I'll never will forget, the Holy Spirit said to me, *"Many of these people achieved their success without me. Imagine what I can do with you if you are faithful to me."* For the first time in my life, I saw real people living real dreams. Right then I told myself, *"If they can do it. I can do it."*

I believe one of the major keys to success is, you have to deal with all the negativity that was deposited into your mindset throughout your growing up years and ask yourself the question, *"Why not me? Why only them and not me? I refuse to become a victim of the negativity that was deposited into my spirit!"* A long time ago, I dreamed about something I didn't see, but now I'm standing in the reality of it, and see it face to face.

One of the things that helped me achieve everything I have accomplished so far is, I saw it! If you can see it, you can achieve it.

CHAPTER THREE

SAVED AT EIGHT

September 27, 1962 was the day God brought me to this earth. Lord willing, on my next birthday, which is a few weeks away as of this writing, I will be sixty-two years old. This signals that I have been a Believer, a Christian for more than fifty-five years.

Looking back on my childhood, I asked myself what salvation looked like and what it meant for an eight-year-old, through the eyes of a child. I'm not sure I gave my heart to Christ because of love or because of fear. In those days the preachers preached hell fire and brimstone. If you did not give your heart to Jesus and if you didn't come out of your sin, you would burn in hell. So, as children and young people, we would go down to the altar and I mean we would just cry, *"God don't punish us! God, don't burn us in hell!"* We would go at it, and the altar workers would pray for us. We repented of our sins and, yes, accepted Jesus into our hearts. We were saved but lived in fear. Every time we did something wrong, we had to get saved all over again and ended up back at the altar Sunday after Sunday, week after week. Back then church was our life! Sunday morning service, Sunday afternoon service, Sunday night service, Bible study, prayer band, and Friday night service. I mean it was always church, church, church! How does a poor family go to church all day Sunday? I'll tell you. After the first service, my mom would go to the store and buy spam, potted meat, tater chips, some bread, maybe some soda or something, and she'd make her sandwiches between church services. That's how we did it.

I always had a special love for God, but didn't really quite understand Him even though I started preaching at the early age of eight. What my grandfather and mother gave me, I preached.

We mimicked the life people in the church demonstrated. As I got older, I began to understand that serving God out of fear was not proper. You serve God out of love because the Bible says, *"For God so loved the world that he gave his only begotten son that whosoever believeth in him should not perish but have everlasting life."* As an adult I also understood that we serve God and love God because in the midst of our sin, God gave the best gift He had, which was his Son. Not to mention, when you serve God out of love, it is not a yoke, nor a taskmaster. It comes from the genuine stream of love from your heart to God. You feel it in your heart. If you did anything that displeased Him it wasn't about you being judged, it wasn't about you being condemned, you just didn't want to break His heart.

One of the things I remember about being saved at such a young age is we were like a sponge and easy to be indoctrinated. Interestingly, I knew, but I didn't know. We assumed, but I guess the older we got, the more we figured out our pastor could not read. So that probably explained why he oftentimes preached the same thing over and over again. I remember one frightening message we were so afraid to hear him preach. He would always say, *"The axe is at the root of the tree and if you don't live right God is going to cut you down!"* As a child I'm picturing God like Paul Bunyan with his axe on his shoulder looking for us to commit a sin to destroy us, but that is not correct! The Bible says, *"The Lord…is not willing that any should perish but that all should come to repentance."* God is long-suffering to us. Oh Lord my God, it is amazing when you're saved as a child. I think you spend more time being traumatized because every time you go to church it's like, *"Oh my God, what did I do now?"* It seemed you could never live good enough and never be good enough. If you even hummed a line of a secular song you were going to hell. You already know my favorite artist was Michael Jackson. Listen, I could sing every song Michael Jackson sang, *"ABC, Easy as 123,"* and *"I'm going back to Indiana."* My admiration for Michael stemmed from him doing what I always wanted to do, music and singing. You didn't really see that in the church. We always saw choirs. The choir I sang in as a young person was called the Sunshine Band. They didn't know it but every time they gave me a song to lead, I used Michael Jackson as my motivation. The choir was the Jackson Five and I was Michael Jackson!

We had some good times and some really bad times growing up as kids being saved. We saw a lot of things we could not explain. I think one of the most traumatizing things for me was, I used to go to sleep in church all the time, and my momma used to fuss at me, *"You're always going to sleep! Wake up, stay up!"* One night we were in church service, and I had fallen asleep. Church was dismissed but no one woke me up. What they did was have everybody go to the back of the church and then cut all the lights off. Everyone was still inside the church and my mom started calling my name, *"Norman, Norman!"* I can't believe they did that to me! When I woke up and I saw nothing but pitch black, I just knew I was in that church by myself. I screamed to high heaven, and they cut the lights on. Everybody was in the back of the church just laughing at me. I tell you what though, I never went to sleep in church again!

In the New Testament scriptures, one of the ways Jesus described the Kingdom was using the likeness of a child, *"Unless you are converted and become as little children, you will by no means enter into the kingdom of heaven."* He was referring to childlike faith, the ability of children to believe without comprehension. Oftentimes no matter what mom or dad said, we believed it, just because they said it. As you grow older, you look for evidence and you look for proof. Being saved at eight years old, my faith was easy to be molded and shaped. At the time, I did not quite understand the power of God, the Holy Spirit but I knew something was different. I could feel and sense the love of God. I felt there was something different imprinted in my life, and that I had been chosen and called by God Himself. God was preserving me as a child, similar to how He did with Moses when his mother hid him in a basket and put him on the Nile River. Later in life God used him to impact the Kingdom of God by being the Deliverer for the nation of Israel. I'm not equating myself to that level, but however God uses you to impact the lives of people, you are valuable to Him.

God Protected Me

There were times I felt really sick when I was in 5th and 6th grades. I don't know why and never told my mom or anyone. I could be outside on the playground and all of a sudden, the world started to spin up and stand still. My stomach would hurt like crazy, and I'd be bent over and I mean I'd be feeling like I was going to faint. Somehow though, I knew but didn't know how I knew, that if I could just find a piece of candy or something sweet, in just a moment or two I'd feel better. Later in my early twenties, I discovered I had diabetes. The same symptoms I experienced in my twenties I remember experiencing in 5th and 6th grades. I was diabetic as a child yet throughout all those years, God protected me. There were several times I would pray and ask God for things. I remember the preacher saying that sometimes we pray without expectation. Sometimes it happened and many times it didn't. But now that I'm older and I look back over my life, I'm telling you what I do know. I can't explain it, but God was with me. He protected me, He kept and guided me, in a childlike simplistic way. One Christmas, we, being very poor, didn't really get a lot for Christmas. I still wanted some cap guns and *Sesame Street* characters. Christmas Eve was about two or three days away. We were out in the country living at my grandfather's house where we took care of the chickens. One of my brothers named Johnny, rest his soul, is in heaven now. Well, I hope he is. He was something else! Anyway, he came home drunk that night, went to bed with a cigarette and dropped it. You can imagine what I'm going to say next, right? Well, the house caught fire and Mama and everybody started screaming, *"Get out of the house! Get out of the house!"* I'm telling you that room was filled with smoke! It looked like the whole wall was on fire. My God, I jumped up out of the bed and ran to the front door. I didn't know what to do. I was young and scared to stay in the house, but I was also scared to go outside because it was so dark. It was pitch black out there in the woods. Finally, we all got out of the house and stood there watching this house go up in flames. Because we were so deep in the country it would take the fire department a long time to get there. I stood next to my mom, watching her, hands lifted up and her eyes looking up into heaven, sorrowfully pleading, *"God I'm sorry forgive me. Lord, please forgive me. God I'm sorry."* To this day I often wonder what my mom was asking God to forgive her for. I do know that oftentimes there were men who weren't our father staying at the house, but it seemed normal. It didn't seem immoral or that anything was wrong. But one of the men I remember was a Deacon at the church. Later on in life I learned he tried to molest two of my sisters in that same house. I don't know if that's what she was asking God to forgive her for because after she left my stepdad she never remarried. I always saw a different man, but we never really paid it any attention.

We moved to town into a small two-bedroom house. There were a lot of us, had to be about six or seven of us living in that house. I just knew

Christmas was over. We weren't going to have a Christmas.But God heard my prayer, my little prayer as a child. On Christmas Day we heard a sound coming and it got closer and closer. The doorbell rang, *"Ding, Ding, Ding, Ding, Ding, Ding."* When I went to the window to look outside, I saw a train on wheels! A big old train on wheels. In back of this train, wow, there was a big ol' Christmas tree for us! Apparently, the town did this for us. There was a big Christmas tree, gifts, toys, clothes and everything! When I looked through the gifts, I saw my cap gun and the *Sesame Street* toys. God answers the prayers of children. He preserved me.

The Mike Tyson Punch

There are too many things that I've experienced as a child. Everybody always wanted to fight me in school because I was such a small guy. I was the second shortest person in the whole school. Here's a funny story, there was girl, gosh I can't remember her name. Let's just call her Marianne because that's what she looked like. She was really light-skinned to put it that way and I liked her. I must have been in the 6th grade. One day we were standing in the lunch line, and you know, we'd be showing off. This little White guy passed by. I don't think he meant to, but he bumped into me. Everybody around us said, *"Ooh he hit you, he hit you!"* She's looking at everything and I called myself going to, you know, be bold and bad. So, I walked up to that little boy in front of all these kids and said, *"You pushed me!"* He just stood there, looked at me and didn't say anything. I said, *"I dare you to hit me, I dare you!"* Let me tell you what that little boy did. That boy, and I don't know where it came from, but he punched me like he was Mike Tyson! He knocked me down on the ground and went on about his business. I finally got myself together. Even as a child you learn lessons as you grow, but you can't always have it your way.

One thing I can say, is every step that I took as a child, God was preserving the gift, the anointing and what He had invested in my heart and spirit because of what He knew I would produce one day. He knew I would be preaching to multitudes and thousands and that my voice would be heard around the world. He knew that people would be healed, saved, set free and delivered by the words of my mouth and the songs that were birthed in my spirit. God, I give you praise for that. I thank you that even in my infancy, you preserved me and when the enemy came in like a flood, you lifted up a standard against him. Years later those symptoms I felt as a child would eventually manifest themselves as disease in my body. God, You still brought me through it. God will always bring you through the valley before He gives you a mountaintop experience. Wisdom doesn't come from the mountain; it comes from the valleys of your life. If God were to deliver you from everything, you'd have nothing to say to encourage somebody else. That's what the Bible says, *"For we have not a high priest who cannot be touched with the feeling of our infirmities, but Christ was tempted in all points like as we are yet without sin."* That's why He can identify with our troubles, with our trials, with everything we ever go through because He suffered just like we do. So, as we move in life from infancy to adulthood we have to look at our troubles, trials, and adversities through the eyes of trust. Can God trust you with the trial?

I believe that God plants seed in us in our youth so that over time, as we mature and grow physically, so does the seed He's planted inside of us. When the Bible says that God will give you the desires of your heart, that does not give reference to physical things like a house, or a car, or wealth. It actually refers to giving you something to desire. God will plant something in your heart, He will plant something in your spirit, and you will not even know what's there until it begins to grow like a seed. So, that's where the desire to be a preacher, to be a singer, and to bless people came from. God planted it in me, then He wrapped zeal and desire around it so it would fuel my life. He did that so as I grew it would be my life's pursuit to become what He has predestined. It was preordained for me to be a preacher, even though as a child I didn't understand it, but I knew what I wanted to be. Life began watering the seeds God planted inside of me by watching others and seeing other people do what God had planted inside of me to do. There will be elements in life that will certainly try to uproot every plant, every seed that God has birthed inside of you as a child but in the incubation stage of your life God protects it. He preserves it by surrounding you with people who will keep you covered in prayer, teach you wisdom and help lead and guide you in the scriptures.

Examples vs. In Samples

There are two different ways of learning. Jesus talks about it. Examples and in samples, two different things. An example is a pattern that you should follow. In samples are patterns you should not follow. God places those two types of people in your life. As you are maturing, the seed will become your purpose and your destiny. So, I followed the pastors and leaders in my life, in my infancy stage. Now that I'm an adult, I've come to understand they weren't examples, they were in samples. Patterns I shouldn't follow, things I should not do.

Later in life as I began to grow, God would plant people in my life who would become examples. Examples of integrity, examples of how to live, how to treat people, like Bishop Blake and many other Bishops who God placed in my life as spiritual mentors. When you read the scriptures, you will never hear the word "in sample" connected to Jesus because there's nothing He ever did that you should not do. Jesus has always been an example, and I praise God for the examples He placed in my life. There was an old missionary in the church, Mother Goldsberry. She was a powerful example and a saved woman of God. I mean every word she spoke sounded like God talking through her mouth!

Another example is Reverend Val Miller. He was old and White, but as I became a teenager, I fell in love with this man. He was just like a father and I'm telling you, we were like two peas in a pod. A little Black boy and this White bald-headed man. He was a Mennonite. What does a Mennonite and a Pentecostal have in common? I learned so much from him. He had a heart of gold and loved people. He wasn't afraid to lead people to Jesus anywhere. I don't care where he went, he was going to talk about Jesus, and he was so passionate! He believed in my ministry and my music. When I was in my teens we would go to church services together. One time during the summer we went out in the field, got all these watermelons and put them in the back of a big old truck. We drove to Washington, DC and sold them on the side of the street for $10. He was an example who showed me how to love people, how to become passionate, and how to love God. God used an old White man. Then one day I got a phone call. He was about a mile from his house and had a head-on collision and died. I couldn't believe it! Mennonite funerals and everything were a little different. When I got to the church nobody was there and I'm trying to figure out what's going on. So, I called the one person I knew, who would know what was going on and they never responded. I went to the house where he lived thinking somebody would be there because his wife was still alive, and he had some older children. Nobody was there.

I searched and searched going to every church he had ever taken me to, and to my deep dismay, I couldn't find his funeral. I couldn't say goodbye to him properly. My heart was broken, but his memories and everything he taught me lives on.

One time, for the first time in my life, Reverend Val Miller said, *"Norman, I've got a surprise for you!"* He took me to my first live concert. I saw this artist, this guy, I don't remember who he was. He was standing in front of a bass player, keyboard player, guitar player, and background singers, and was just a singing. Reverend Miller had shown me my future! He kept looking at me and saying, *"That's gonna be you, that's gonna be you!"* He watered my dreams! Always appreciate those who God sends to water your dreams! Never forget! Never forget! It is the pain of the valley, the disappointments of the valley. It is the transitions that you will go through in life in your valley that will help sustain you on your mountain. Know that so you do not become prideful, so that you never believe you're better than anybody else, and that you will always remember that God is the God of the valley and He's the God of the Mountain. The Bible says, *"He that humbles himself shall be exalted but he that exalts himself shall be abased."* God, I thank you for those that you have planted in my life to be examples and also in samples.

CHAPTER FOUR

SERMONS FROM MY MOTHER

It is 3:00 in the afternoon, the school bell rings and it's time to go home. I'm excited because I get to meet up with my friends in the neighborhood! We're going to go play football and just spend some fun time together doing whatever, all over town. I arrived home only to hear my mother say, *"Norman, you've been asked to preach at a church in Maryland or Georgetown or even Virginia."* That meant I couldn't go play with my friends. I would go to my mom's room, and she would give me a sermon to preach. Even though I struggled to read, and I mean I really struggled, I had the gift of memorization. She would tell me the story twice, then she asked me to repeat it.

We lived during the 60s when the church did not embrace women preachers. I believe my mother was actually called to be a preacher, but because the church was so hard on women in the pulpit, she never really developed her gift to preach. When my mother recognized I was called to be a preacher at such a young age, she would preach through me. She gave me scriptures, I'd memorize them, then she would give me questions to answer. I still have my Bible story book my mother used to read to me. At the end of each story were ten questions. She would ask me those questions and if I got them all right, she felt I was ready. On our way to service, my mom would rehearse the sermon I was going to preach with me. What's amazing is I was not nervous, I was excited! I really was! I knew I was born to do this. There was never a time in my life that I doubted or didn't believe I was going to be a preacher.

I can't remember my mother and I talking about life. She was divorced and taking care of many kids. She was busy bringing me back and forth to the different churches where I was to preach, and the next day I'd be right back in school. Passing through the state of Virginia now as an adult, I see how bad it's become. Wow! Particularly in Eastern Shore Virginia, like New Church or Accomack, Virginia. I can still see these churches where I preached as child in my mind to this day. One of the most frightening memories I have while preaching at a church in Virginia was when there were more people outside than inside. The graveyard was located out front, alongside and in the back. To enter into the church, you had to walk along this same graveyard path. I was so scared dead people were going to climb out of those graves and come get me! I guess that's just the mind of a child.

Mama, We Got Bills To Pay

It got to the point where my mother quit her job because of the high demand of me preaching up and down the East Coast. I was preaching so much until one day while at my grandmother's house, I overheard my mom and grandmother having a conversation. My grandmother, Ethel Phillips, told my mother, *"Doris, you are going to kill him, you gotta slow down!"* My mother says, *"Mama, but we got bills to pay."* Every time I preached, even as a small child, I was given what is called a love token, which is basically an offering. The love token would always be presented after I preached by saying, *"We can't pay you for that wonderful message, but this is just a token of our appreciation."* Then they would give me the envelope and I would put it in my pocket. On our way home I would give the envelope to my mother, and she would use it to pay for food, house rent or life's necessities.

Between the ages of eight and eleven, my preaching supported the family. Many of my brothers didn't like me either because I guess they thought our mother cared more about me than them but that was not the case. It was our main financial source for living. So, I preached all the time. One church I preached at was packed to capacity and I started, as the old folks used to say, *"You smellin' yourself."* That meant you were becoming prideful and thinking you're all that. My mom used to tell me, *"God is going to put you to shame. He's going to humble you!"* As a young preacher, I was preaching to packed out churches. You couldn't tell me nothing! I knew I was somebody, not to mention the young girls used to line up just to get a glimpse or shake my hand. Pride was written all over my face. Nowadays as I travel, people always say, *"He's such a humble pastor and man of God."* I can pinpoint the date and time God humbled me. I was preaching at a church celebrating an anniversary. The building was filled to capacity with people from all over the state. About four of my sisters and I sang as my mother played the piano and then I would preach. After we finished singing, I got up to preach, read my scripture and gave my subject. Just before I started to expound on the text I had this urge to go to the bathroom really, really bad. I'm about twelve years old and thinking I couldn't stop and go to the bathroom because I had read my scripture and given my subject. So now, I've got to preach! I thought I could just ignore it, it would go away and I would be okay. Well, about another five minutes into my sermon the urge to use the bathroom was at its all-time high. I was surrounded by preachers behind and on the side of me. Remember now, the place was packed. All of a sudden, I couldn't hold it anymore and a warm liquid started running down the leg of my light-colored suit pants. You could see the wetness. You could hear a pin drop and as I was urinating on myself, it sounded like somebody was pouring water in a bucket. My mother was on the piano looking at me. She's looking at me and I'm looking at her not knowing what to do. I stopped talking and stood there with everybody in the audience wondering what's wrong. But behind me and on the side, they knew because *ohh* they saw it. After I finished using the bathroom on myself, I went to close my Bible and leave out of the church when my mother, from the piano, said to me, *"You stay right there, and you preach!"* Wow! I couldn't believe she said that, but that's what I did. I preached the whole sermon wet from peeing on myself. I can't tell you how embarrassed and humiliated I was. When I finished preaching, I wanted to go sit in the car, but my mother wouldn't let me. You know how they have punch, cake and cookies in the dining hall after the anniversary service? My mom said, *"Come right in here, sit down and eat."* When we were finally on our way home my mom reminded me, *"I told you that God was going to get you!"* Yeah, I just cried and cried and cried and repented. The truth is, I was twelve when that happened. I'm sixty-two now and have never had a problem with pride again!

My mother was a very hard worker. She never shared the challenges she faced as a single mother with twelve children after being divorced from my stepfather. I believe she was looking for love but in all the wrong faces. Every so often we were introduced to a new man who would be around for a while, then disappear. At the same time my mother was still cultivating me as a young preacher, still giving me sermons and taking me to different churches to preach. As a young child, it's difficult to discern what is morally or spiritually right or wrong. You tend to overlook any flaws in your parents' actions because your love for them is so strong.

I don't remember being nurtured by my mother during my youth. Church work always took precedence. Everything was centered around church. While mom was giving me sermons, she was also focused on getting the offerings so we could pay the bills. As I got older, I started thinking, *"This is my money. I'm doing the preaching. Why should I always have to give mom all the money?"* You know what? I would never say that because my momma used to say, *"I will slap the taste out of your mouth!"* I love food too much!

One time I went to preach at this church and after I finished, they gave me the offering. I wanted some sneakers because I got tired of wearing those Bubbles. You know, that's what they called them in school, Bubbles. The kids would always laugh at our clothes and shoes, so I came up with this crazy idea. After I finished preaching, I took $40 out of the offering, put it in my pocket, and closed the envelope. When we got in the car, as usual, I gave mom the envelope. She put it away when we got home and later that night, she called me in the room and said, *"Norman, did you take any money out of this envelope?"* Lord, have mercy, I was so scared. I knew better not to say yes because I was gonna get a whoopin', so I said, *"No ma'am, no ma'am!"* But dummy me, what I didn't know is that the offering amount was written on the envelope, and it was missing $40. She showed me the envelope and she said, *"Well, how come this is what it says? I know they got it right."* Then Mama got that deep, spiritual look in her eyes like she was looking right through me, *"You took it didn't you? Didn't you take it!?"* That's when I broke down and confessed the truth. She said, *"Why did you steal the money?"* I told her, *"Because I wanted to get me a pair of sneakers."* She replied, *"Well, we've got bills."* I gave her the money back, and don't think I got a whooping for stealing the money. The whooping I got was for lying. Think about that for a moment. I got a whooping for taking my own money.

Marked As A Small Child

Another memorable experience I had preaching a sermon my mother had given me was the first time the presence of a demon manifested itself through a woman in the congregation. I don't remember the name of the church, but it was full. I was up preaching, and the woman stood up and started walking down the aisle and talking with a deep, dark voice. I just stood there, and people were looking around. I didn't know what to do, but other preachers who did know, got up and started praying and casting the devil out of her. When they were done, I finished preaching. Demons are real! As I look back over my life, I see now how God shielded me. He protected me from the forces of Satan. Satan saw what God was going to produce in my life. He knew God was going to use my mouth to sing and to preach the Kingdom of God, so even as a small child I was marked. Satan and his demons always wanted to destroy my life, but God protected and shielded me.

Through all of the things I experienced as a child of God, I believe God guarded me from things that would have damaged me mentally. He knew I would need my mind and didn't want me dealing with issues in my childhood that would damage me mentally. *God, I thank You for that. I thank You that in spite of there being several molestation attempts on my life as a child, you shielded me from it.* Even though I didn't know what it was, I recognized it was wrong. God either wouldn't let it happen, or I knew it wasn't right. He has been so good to me.

The sermons my mom gave me to preach, I called Bible stories. Some of my favorite Bible stories were about David, but particularly Joseph. When I used to preach about Joseph my God, it's like I saw it myself. Joseph was hated by his brothers you know, and eventually he would become the second in command of the Pharaoh's Kingdom. God used him in a great way. I saw how God would allow me to grow and begin using my life. I don't know why my brothers hated me so much. Maybe it was because I was a half-brother, I don't know, but out of all of my brothers I did have one brother who didn't live at home when I was young. He was already grown and living in New York. He would come home every once in a while, and what I loved about him was anytime he came home, he would always bring me an instrument. One time he brought me a saxophone, then he brought me a bass guitar. Another year he brought me a lead guitar, and a set of drums. There were two to three years in between each time he came bearing these musical gifts, but my goal was to learn how to play them. So by the time he came back I'd know how to play them. I didn't realize that even back then, God was using my half-brother to help develop my musicianship.

There was always a piano in the house, an upright that always needed tuning. It sounded like those pianos in the western saloons back in the day. All of these things eventually blended together to develop who I am today. Music in my family growing up was really big. Several of my brothers and sisters played piano and every one of them felt their own songs were amazing, but I guess I was the one who had it in my heart and spirit. Music is what I wanted to do for a living. No one in my family really thought that one day I would have music played and heard around the world! They never saw me ministering in concerts or as a recording artist. In 1992, my family heard my first recording, *Press Toward the Mark* on the "Saints in Praise" album produced by West Angeles Church of God in Christ. I was living in California at the time, and they couldn't believe their little brother was doing exactly what he said he always wanted to do since childhood. I am truly, truly grateful.

We were somewhere deep in the state of Maryland and on our way to another church where I would be preaching. It was a night service, and we were returning home pretty late. This trip was different because Deacon Sonny from the church was with me and my mother. He was driving the car, and it never dawned on me that they were actually seeing each other. I just thought he was a Deacon from the church volunteering to take us to preach. So, we're on our way for me to preach. Mom is rehearsing my sermon in the car by asking me questions about my text and my subject. She was correcting some of the storyline and as we're getting closer to the church, constantly reminding me to talk loudly and preach good, saying things like, "*You got this!*"

We had a wonderful service that everyone enjoyed but here's the thing. I was too young to understand what was really going on. Mr. Sonny was not married to my mom, but he was another one of those men we would often see around. Eventually, like all the others, he was gone. This must have been one of the most horrific things that ever happened to me as a child preacher. I never talked about it, never told anyone until now. On our way back home, I remember we stopped in this town called Seville in Delaware, located just at Maryland's state line. I remember like it was yesterday because it was so upsetting. I must have been ten years old, maybe even younger. We pulled into the driveway of this very small house. It had one bedroom, a living room, and a kitchen. Walking in the front door, you're in the living room. Keep straight and you're in the bedroom. If you go to the right and around the corner, there's a small kitchen. The whole house was furnished with old tables, couches and chairs, like back in the 60s. Now the craziest thing about it was the graveyard across the street. As soon as we pulled up, I saw that big old graveyard and, boy oh boy, I was not happy about that! I was a scary kid growing up. Everything scared me, but when I saw that graveyard, oh my God!

When we walked into the house, I noticed my mom went right in the bedroom and shut the door. Mr. Sonny reached in his bag and pulled out a toy. An 18-wheeler truck! Oh man, that thing was a bad little rounded, double 18-wheeler, like one of those trucks that carry gas. He got down on the floor and rolled the truck around while I sat there looking because I wanted to play with it. By this time my mom came out of the room holding a blanket that she spread on the floor like a pallet. While I'm looking at the truck and listening to Mr. Sonny, I'm also seeing what my mom is doing. I'm thinking, *"Now I know what a pallet is, that means this is where you're going to sleep."* I'm looking at the pallet, I'm looking at the truck, I'm thinking about the graveyard and I'm thinking, *"Now, I know they're not going to go inside this room and leave me out here."* Mr. Sonny finally gave me the truck and said, *"Here you play with it."* I started playing with the truck as my mom walked back in the room but before she left, she said, *"This is where you are going to sleep, Norman."* All I was thinking about was the graveyard but didn't say anything because we didn't talk back. Mr. Sonny went on in the room and my mom got me to lay down before following him. Before you know it, I'm crying and when she went in that room and shut that door, my God, it's almost like I can feel it to this day! I thought every dead body in that graveyard was gonna come through that front door! So, I curled up at the door, cried all night long and never went to sleep. Every time something would move or shake, I thought it was somebody. Mom and Mr. Sonny heard me crying and sometimes screaming but they never came and got me. When the sun came up, they finally came out of the room. I did not sleep all night and don't even remember what happened. We left that house, and I guess he took us home. It never dawned on me what they were doing in that room. I was a child preacher preaching the gospel and my mom was basically seeing a man, neither of them married. Thinking about this as an adult, I believe she was just looking for love in all the wrong places. My mother was such an abused woman with all these kids. All I know is I had preached that night and lived a nightmare in that house. No one ever knew. After church service everybody's shaking my hand and giving me hugs. I'm this little young man hugging everybody. They were so excited saying things like, *"Oh my Lord, God is going to use you!"* Little did I know the nightmare awaiting me after that service. What I do know is God kept me.

My mother died young in her early fifties. I was sitting next to her in church one day when she had a stroke. I believe it was the stresses in life that took her, all the things she suffered and went through. Every time we were scheduled to preach I would always ask my mom, *"Okay, what are we going to preach this time?"* This particular time, my God, I remember her saying, *"You've got to get your message yourself. You gotta pray and ask God to give it to you."* I cried like a baby because I didn't know what to preach, I didn't know what to say. She told me to go in her room, lay down and put my head in the Bible.

She may have made that up, but I thought it would work. I fell asleep, woke up and still didn't have a sermon, but eventually God did impress something on my heart. The title God provided was *Abraham and Isaac.* My grandfather would sometimes rehearse my sermons with me too if my mom was too busy, but after that day God impressed upon my heart the sermon I would preach. That was the last time I got an assignment from my mother.

Growing up in the church, within the youth department, they had what is called a platform service. A Platform Service is when they let the young ministers in the church preach for about five minutes. Sometimes it would be about four or five different ministers. Of course, the sermons my mother had given me, I had memorized and sometimes used them during that time of preaching. It amazed me because the responses I got from the congregation were unbelievable. You could tell there was a special anointing on my life through my presentation, even as a small child in church. My pastor recognized it and from time to time would let me preach during the church's main service. When I did, it was powerful and by this time God was giving me my own sermons. I must have been about twelve years old. From the ages of eight to twelve my mother and grandfather gave me my sermons. Now I was old enough to craft my own. God would place an inspiration or a theme in my heart. Then I'd find scriptures to go with that theme and use to expound on. My pastor licensed me as a minister at twelve years old at Holy Trinity Church of God in Christ in Millsboro, Delaware.

I would wonder from time to time. We would see the pastor at the house and not just after church on Sundays. He would be around, and I was too young to understand what that was about. I don't want to speculate but I do remember one time he came to our house. He drove over when my mom wasn't there. She was working or out doing something. We noticed the pastor was drunk. I mean he was really under the influence of alcohol. We tried to make him leave but what was crazy to us is that he knew where he could lay down and get some sleep to work that off of him. He woke up several hours later and left. We could tell he was still kind of drunk because he backed out of the driveway, hit the mailbox and broke it. I believe he had a drinking problem. He was one of the nicest men you would ever want to meet in the world, but he was wrestling with alcoholism.Because he strived as an alcoholic for so many years, I believe he developed some form of cancer. Eventually he died, and my mother started going to another church in Bridgeville, Maryland called Creative Faith Temple Church of God in Christ.

He's Yours Now

I must have been about twelve years old at the time, maybe even thirteen because I was right on the cusp of those teenage years. Once we joined the church, my mother told our new pastor, Bishop Foreman, *"He's yours now. I've taken him as far as I can. So, I need you to take him under your wing and be a father to him. Teach him and help him continue to grow and become the preacher God wants him to be."*

I thought Bishop E.T. Foreman liked me and then other times I don't believe he did. The thought crossed my mind that he was jealous of me. I was so anointed as a child. I could play the organ, was a musician, could direct a choir and then preach. There were times when I would preach, I was reminded of the song of David that says, *"Saul has killed his thousands and David his tens of thousands."* Because Saul felt that the people attributed more to David than himself, he was jealous. Could it be possible that my spiritual leader, my father, my new pastor was jealous because of my ability to communicate the Word of God and preach it in such a way that people were mesmerized and so excited? Sometimes his treatment was confusing because it felt like someone who loved me but was jealous of me at the same time. He also recommended me to become an elder and ordained me at nineteen years old.

By this time my mother had suffered a mild stroke and was dealing with high blood pressure and diabetes. When I felt the leading of the Lord to birth a church at twenty years old, I went to my pastor to let him know. He turned against me and isolated me from the church and the young people. He told them they better not ever go visit my church. I was so hurt.

I remember pushing my mother in a wheelchair into the first church service at New Hope Church of God in Christ. I witnessed my mom raise her hands during service, praising and thanking God. I was remembering the day God called me to pastor at eight years old up until I started pastoring my first church at twenty years old. God allowed her to see it! My mother came to the first service and became very, very ill. Apparently, she had another stroke or even a heart attack and that's when she died.

From time to time people tell me that I'm a great storyteller, but the truth is I got it from my mother. When she used to give me my sermons, she would tell them to me as little stories and even dramatize them. So, I picked that up and began to do the same. It's been years now since my mother's passing. But even now, from time to time, when I'm facing crises and challenges in life, I can hear my Mama saying, *"Repeat this after me..."* and it would be one of her sermons. There was one sermon where she talked about love and how important it was to love everybody and not judge them, no matter who they are. She was so convincing.

My mother had twelve children, six boys, six girls and I'm the baby boy. We were a big family, and we had each other. When my mother cooked dinner, it sometimes looked like she was cooking up a Thanksgiving meal. Where she got the money I have no idea, I just know that we ate everyday. I had my little red wagon and don't even remember who bought it for me. During this time there were no EBT cards or food stamps, but if you were on welfare like we were, you would go to the National Guard base once a month. I would pull my red wagon with my mom, and we would get in this long, long line of people. As we got closer to the front they would load my wagon down with meat, spam, powdered eggs, big blocks of butter, a sweet big old can of peanut butter, and milk. We would take it back home and use that to help cook the other food we had. We were poor, but I didn't know it because we still survived.

Now that my mother is gone, sometimes I can still hear her repeating those sermons to me. One in particular was John 3:16, *"For God so loved the world that he gave his only begotten son that whosoever believeth in him should not perish but have everlasting life."* She was teaching me how much God loves us and how He forgives us for all of our sins. I guess my mom, in a different kind of way, was more than just a mother. She was my *Moses,* she was my *Abraham,* she was my *Elijah,* and I thank God today that I am who I am. Even though my mother did not live a perfect life, even though she did things that were not pleasing in the sight of God, I know she always made sure I was prepared when it came time for me to preach. Thank you for the sermons, mom.

CHAPTER FIVE

MY FATHER DISOWNED ME

I'm between the ages of eleven and twelve. I'm a very popular child evangelist on the East Coast traveling from Delaware to Virginia to North Carolina, Baltimore, New Jersey and Washington DC, just to name a few. Once a year we traveled to Kingston, North Carolina for me to preach at Saint Matthews Baptist Church. Everywhere I went as a child, the churches were always packed to capacity. I used to ask my mother, *"Why does this pastor always cry when I finish preaching?"* She would answer, *"He just loves you."*

I remember overhearing people say things like, *"He looks just like our Pastor Earl E. Garner."* I never placed much thought on it because I knew he couldn't be my dad. My dad was an alcoholic and when my mom left him, we moved to Delaware. My dad was my abuser so the thought of Reverend Garner being my father never crossed my mind. People even said things straight to me like, *"Wow you look just like our pastor!"* I mean yes, we both were dark-skinned, but I didn't know anything about his mannerisms and other similar characteristics. I think it was right around the third visit during our third year ministering in North Carolina that my grandmother traveled with us. We were upstairs at my sister's house getting dressed when my grandma came to me and said, *"Norman, your dad is downstairs."* I was so shocked and surprised. Even though he was an abuser and was more than mean to me, I can't explain why, but I just wanted to see him. Actually, I was happy to see him but when I went downstairs, I didn't see him. Pastor Earl E. Garner was there to pick us up and take us to church. I spoke to him, he spoke back to me, but I was looking for James Hutchins, my stepdad who I thought was my dad at the time. I went back upstairs and told my grandma, *"Grandma, my daddy's not downstairs."* She said, *"Yes, he is, that preacher your daddy. He's your real dad."* I didn't say anything. After we got dressed, my grandma, my mom and, I can't remember who else was with us, got in the car. The pastor was driving us to church, and I was just staring at him and thinking about what my grandmother said, but I didn't say anything.

When we arrived at the church, we got out of the car and went to the office. As we were preparing to leave the office for the sanctuary, I heard one of the mothers ask him, *"Pastor, is it true that this is your son?"* I was standing right next to him when he answered her, *"No, mother, this is an evangelist from Delaware."* I believed my grandmother when she told me, but when he told the church mother that I was just an evangelist from Delaware, I couldn't believe it. I don't even know how I preached that day at his church, but I got through it, and I never told him I knew he was my biological father. I paid attention to the different things people were saying, and I put two and two together. It's interesting though, in my twelve-year-old mind it was confusing because I'm asking myself, *"How could this be? How is it even possible?"* I had a million questions going through my mind, but what I do know is when we left and were on our way back to Delaware, I didn't tell my mom I knew. What I did tell her was I didn't want to go back to that church ever again. She asked me why. I knew why but I made up something. I can't remember what, but eventually she found out. We really never had any more conversations about it because back in those days you didn't talk about things, you just brushed them under a rock.

Years later, after my mother passed, I moved to California to go to Bible college and a total change of life. An old friend, who was in the Navy and stationed in Fontana, California, called me and said, *"Norman, you should move to Los Angeles! There are great opportunities out here for you!"* So, I did, and he put me up. He gave me a place to live and in 1994 I began working in a warehouse. My biological father died and out of respect to the family I went to the funeral in North Carolina. I was amazed because there were hundreds and hundreds of people and had to be over a thousand bishops from all over the state as well as city officials.

I walked in with the family because by this time certain people knew that I was his son. I could hear people saying, *"Oh my God, you look just like him,*" and I just looked straight ahead. I sat next to a young man only to discover that he was my biological brother, and he was a twin. I didn't know I had twin brothers. Not me, but I had twin brothers. I met eight other sisters and several sisters and brothers between my mother's twelve children, the father's twelve children, me being one of seven out of wedlock.

I Have 31 Brothers and Sisters

I'm sitting there listening to these people talk about the things he had done and yet he disowned me as his son. He never knew, standing in the hallway, that I knew he was my dad and heard him tell someone I wasn't his son. I was listening to his accomplishments and how he helped so many families and so many different people, yet he disowned me as a son. Now, I have to backtrack for a moment. I remember when I became an adult, he knew that I knew he was my dad but he never reached out to talk to me. I knew I had several sisters and met them even before the funeral, not to mention I look more like them on his side than I do on my mom's side. I took it upon myself to go and visit during Christmas because his wife reached out to me and told me how the family always comes together for Christmas. That's something my family on my mom's side never did. So I was curious, and thought this might be an opportunity to talk to him. So, I went for the Christmas celebration. When I saw him, he spoke to me, I spoke to him and that was pretty much it. My sisters on his side were so glad to see me because I'm the baby brother on their side. By this time, I'm doing music, and they know some of my songs. It's like they have a little celebrity in the family and I'm trying to decide if their happiness is genuine or because of my success.

My oldest sister, we'll call her EJ, claims she remembered when her daddy was making me. He would visit my mom's house while my stepdad was in jail and tell her to stay in the car because she was young, and he had to go in and pray. She said by the time he came back to the car she was asleep. I guess he was in there praying and laying on of hands.

Being there at the party was interesting because I knew I was part of their family. I looked more like them than I did anybody on my mother's side, yet I felt no connection. I wanted some answers, but was afraid. As I said earlier, we grew up during a time when you didn't ask questions. This man walked around that house and did all the stuff he was doing and I'm sitting there thinking, "*You don't think you need to say something to me?*"

He was a good cook, and I know I got it from him. For the holidays he cooked a pig. A whole pig! He had dug a deep hole outside to build a pit and created a grill. He wrapped it with coal and wood for the fire, and that's where he laid the pig. It would take hours to cook. Everybody's inside joking, laughing and having a great time. He was quiet, just listening. I remember seeing him get up to go outside and check on the pig to flip it and you know, do whatever he needed to do. I decided to walk out behind him and stand there watching him open up the foil and brushing some sauce on it. He wasn't talking so I thought I'd ask some questions. I said, "*What's that you're putting on the pig?*" He said, "*This is my secret sauce.*" I remember how he boasted about his sauce and what he was doing. I'm thinking to myself, "*I just want one question answered.*" That was, "*Why did you disown me, why have you never reached out to me? I came to your church and preached as a child! You knew you were my dad, and you never said a word. I saw your tears. Were they tears of joy? Were they tears of sorrow? Or were they tears of guilt? I never felt love from you. I never knew you! What do I tell my sons when they ask me to tell them about you?*" Of course, he didn't say anything. We just stood around the makeshift fire pit speaking barely a word. I went back inside the house, and the rest of the weekend just went by.

When I returned to California, I regretted ever going. Now I'm sitting at the funeral, looking at the casket and listening to these people talk about a man who had done so much for others than he did for me as his own son. I remember walking up to look inside of his casket for the last time to find that he looked like me in my mid-twenties. It seemed like I was looking at myself after giving my life to Christ at eight years old preaching up and down the East Coast. Now I'm bitter at God, but too afraid to speak out what was in my mind and in my heart. "*I don't understand how I could give my life to You at such an early age. People were being blessed and coming to You, and yet my own biological father disowned me as his son.*"

The funeral is over now, and everybody is back home. I was new to California, living in Fontana and working at the warehouse for Advance Business Forms as a forklift driver. Still dealing with what I had left in Kingston, North Carolina, I'm trying to move on with my life but in the back of my mind, I still hear the Holy Spirit saying, *"I'm going to place men in your life to father you, to mentor you, to teach and help you grow."* I started singing songs I'd written at different churches trying to establish myself as a singing artist. God would have it one day when I was in Banning, California singing at a church, as I finished and was walking back to my seat, this gentleman gave me a business card and said, *"Give me a call."* My God, I looked up and couldn't believe it was Andraé Crouch, one of my musical mentors and a giant in the gospel music industry. Being so excited, I called him, and he invited me to visit his father's church. Bishop Benjamin Crouch was a giant in the Kingdom and chairman of the pastors and elders counsel for the Church of God in Christ. There were over six million members not to mention he was also a Jurisdictional Bishop in the state of California. Bishop Crouch was a powerful man! He embraced me right from the beginning, me and my family. Our children were small at the time. We had three children, two boys and a girl—Norman, Anthony and Tiffany. Bishop Crouch invited me back to preach, then he invited me back to do a revival Monday through Friday. Two nights into the revival, Andraé Crouch played the organ for me, and it was surreal. At the end of the first week, Bishop Crouch didn't even ask me, but he asked the congregation, *"You guys want to go another week?"* Everybody was clapping and saying yes. The church was packed every night, so he said, *"Alright son, well we gotta do another week."* I was driving from Fontana and wasn't put up in a hotel, given a transportation stipend or anything. We drove from Fontana to Christ Memorial Church of God in Christ in Pacoima, which is approximately one hundred and forty miles round trip and a little over a two-hour drive. In week two, our car broke down and they sent somebody to come get us. Bishop Crouch got up at the end of the service and said, *"Well you know the preacher can't come to the revival if he doesn't have a car. His car broke down."* A lady stood up and said, *"I have a car, I have a car. I'll give it to him."* I'm telling you it was a 1968 Mustang! That thing was clean, and I couldn't believe she gave us a Mustang!

I started going to the Christmas parties and spending time with Andraé and Sandra at Andraé's house. I was like a new addition to the family, but I had my eyes on Bishop Benjamin Crouch, Andraé's dad. I believe he was the first man God placed in my life for me to watch. I watched how he did business and dealt with people. One day Andraé came to me and said, *"My daddy loves you. He has a church near Palm Springs, California and wants you to pastor that church."* I really don't think I was ready to be a pastor, but because Andraé told me he would work with me musically and was arranging a lot of my music, I felt I couldn't say no. If I said no, he probably wouldn't help me, so I said yes. The church was in Banning, right outside of Palm Springs. My wife and I, and our three kids moved to a beautiful church in Banning. There weren't many people, maybe about twenty-five members. Banning was a desert place at the time so we would travel back and forth to Pacoima.

Most of the time we were in Banning working with the church and things got bad for us. There were no jobs, and I wasn't on salary at the church. We applied for welfare, food stamps and general assistance but I couldn't understand why they wouldn't help us. There were several times when church members would either give us money for groceries or help us financially. I don't know how Bishop Crouch found out about it, but it got back to him and that's when I started seeing a side of him I didn't know existed. He fussed at me like I had done something so wrong. He said, *"These are my people, they're not supposed to help you!"* I said, *"Bishop, but you know we don't have money or food."* He then commenced to saying, *"Get a job!"* I replied, *"Bishop, there's no jobs out here."* He repeated, *"Well, these are my people."* I believe I know why God allowed me to meet Bishop Crouch. Some of the lessons He wanted me to learn was, in being a preacher and being a pastor you have to be compassionate. Bishop Crouch was one way in public, but he dealt with me in a different way. I was very quiet about it and never really said anything. I often wondered if Andre and Sandra even knew. I sat down with Andraé one time and told him how I was out there trying to pastor the church, how there were no people out there, and that my family was suffering. He didn't volunteer to help or anything, which left me totally confused.

I'm trying to figure out what to do. Another lesson I learned was, you can connect to influential and famous people but if you're out of the will of God, it can't work. I made up my mind as the father of my children and the husband of my wife, I had to do something. So, one day I made a decision to resign as Pastor. We just got through moving from Banning but there was no way we could survive. I thought maybe I would go back to Fontana or even thought about moving back home to Delaware. I called Bishop Crouch and said, *"Bishop, I'm going to have to resign."* I was not prepared for what came next. He said, *"You can't leave."* I'm thinking, *"Did he say what I thought he just said?"* He made it clear, *"No, you can't leave."* I rebutted with, *"But with all due respect, I've got to take care of my family and it's not happening out here."* With venom coiled in his throat he said, *"Do you know who I am? I am Bishop Benjamin Crouch!"* He knew I was a young preacher growing up in the Church of God in Christ. He continued, *"If you leave this church, you will not be able to preach anywhere!"* In other words, he's saying, *"I'll shut you down!"* I'm telling you, as a young man, I couldn't believe I was hearing this from someone of that magnitude! I had an opportunity to meet my mentor, Andraé Crouch but it was unbelievable to see how fast things turned within four years! I do remember saying, *"Bishop, with all due respect I am going to have to resign because I've got to take care of my family."* That was it. He just hung up. I went home broken, disappointed and feeling like a failure, not to mention thinking about moving back home.

My mind was spiraling with all these thoughts. Could I get the house back I was renting? We had already sold all of our furniture. Another challenge I faced was leaving my church and the community that had supported me. They threw a big farewell celebration filled with encouragement, saying things like, *"You're going to California, and you're going to make it big! We believe in you, your music, and your talent."* But now, I found myself heading back home, feeling like I've failed, with my head hanging low. We stayed in the house for about a week trying to make up my mind what I wanted to do. A day or so later I went back to the church to get the rest of my things out of the office and while I packing, this big black Mercedes pulled up. It was Andraé and Sandra Crouch. They came in the office and saw what I was doing. Andraé sat down in the chair, shaking his head in disappointment. Sandra, like a mother and spokesman lit into me. You could tell that she was her father's daughter. She said, *"You hurt my dad! You hurt my dad! What are you gonna do now? You had a bird nest on the ground. We were going to take you around the world!"* I said, *"But I can't feed my family. I'm not interested in the world if I can't feed my family."* Andraé was sitting there saying, *"You hurt my dad. You hurt me."* I'm thinking to myself, *"You guys are rich and famous, and you know there's nothing out here."* Then I remember Sandra asking me, *"What are you going to do now?"* I looked at her and said, *"I don't know, but I'm going to get back in the will of God."* By that time, I knew the reason why

I was suffering the way I was and that is because I was out of God's will. What I've learned about being in the will of God is like the glory cloud God used for the Children of Israel. That cloud led them to the land of Canaan. The Bible says in the Book of Exodus, *when the cloud stood still, they stood still, when the cloud moved, they moved.* It was very important for them to follow the cloud. The Bible says there was a cloud by day and a pillar of fire by night. God used the cloud to guide and direct them. There were always three things present in the cloud: the presence of God, the anointing of God, and the provision of God. As long as the Children of Israel stayed under that cloud, those three things were always visible. I knew I was not in the will of God because my family was suffering.

After telling Sandra I was going to get back in the will of God, I got my box with my things and left. They also left and that was the last time I would hear from Bishop Crouch, Andraé and Sandra for years. I went back home and stayed in the house praying and repenting to God. My wife started suggesting we visit West Angeles Church, almost one hundred miles away from where we were. I didn't know Bishop Blake or anything about West Angeles Church, nor anyone there. Still, every week my wife would say, *"Let's visit West Angeles,"* because she heard about the church. One day I finally said okay. Why not? I was already determined that I'm going back home to Delaware where I knew I could get a job and take care of my family. To appease her I decided, *"Hey, why not? Let's go to West Angeles."*

It's Sunday morning and we're driving to Los Angeles from Banning to visit West Angeles Church. I'd never been to hear a pastor I didn't know or heard about. We were so amazed when we got there because we stood outside in a line like you're getting on a roller coaster. I was told this was the third service. I couldn't believe it and had never seen anything like this in my entire life. We finally made it inside; I mean we just made it inside the sanctuary. There were three or four overflow areas! I guess God wanted me in the sanctuary. The choir and music were powerful! I'm looking at the choir and the band, seeing in reality what I've always dreamed of doing. The people were praising God and, oh my Lord, I just couldn't find words. Then this tall, handsome and eloquent gentleman walks to the podium and starts preaching. Mesmerized is the only word that comes to mind as I am listening to Bishop Charles E. Blake preach in person for the first time in my life. The craziest thing was there were thousands of people in that room and I felt like he was preaching to an audience of one. It felt like the only two people in that room was me and Bishop Blake. The sermon he preached spoke to my life. He talked about being disappointed by people and feeling like a failure. He talked about being out of the will of God. I mean he was reading my mail! After the sermon, he did an altar call. He said, *"If you feel like you're out of the will of God I want to pray for you."* Of course, by that time I was already prepared to go back to Delaware but, I went to the altar. As soon as I got to that altar, the Holy Spirit spoke to me and said, *"I finally got you where I want you. Do not leave until I tell you."* I came back to my seat and told my wife what the Holy Spirit said. She was excited, the kids were excited and we joined church the next Sunday.

Now we're living in Banning, going to a church in Los Angeles almost on hundred miles one way, two hundred miles round trip. We're still on welfare food stamps but I was being fed. I was so thirsty for God, for the Word and just being in that atmosphere. We drove every Sunday. Not only did we go to church, but we went to all three morning services. After the third service, we would go to McDonald's or Kentucky Fried Chicken and get the kids some food and drive back to the church. We parked across the street, next door to West Angeles' Christian Academy in the gated parking lot. The children could eat and then play until 6:30 p.m., when it was time for YPWW and then on to the 7:00 p.m. service.

He Called Me Marvin

That was our schedule for the next year and a half. We even attended Wednesday night Bible study. We were there! The kids loved it and were involved in the youth department. I started singing and ministering around the city here and there. Elder Green, the Assistant Pastor did my new members interview, so I never really had a chance to meet Bishop Blake one-on-one. Matter of fact, when I did meet him, he got my name wrong. He didn't call me Norman, he called me Marvin. I don't know why, and I didn't correct him either. He called me Marvin for a whole year until one day he said, *"Wait a minute, your name is not Marvin, it's Norman!"* I laughed and said, *"Yes, sir, that's the name my momma gave me!"*

After about a year and a half or so, I'm home fixing our welfare breakfast, is what I called it cause I bought it with the food stamps. Then the telephone rang. I answered it and the voice says, *"Hello Elder Hutchins, this is Charles Blake."* I said wait a minute. I didn't even know he knew my name. Next he said, *"The Lord laid it on my heart to ask you to preach this Wednesday night for our Wednesday night service."* I said, *"Yes sir!"* I couldn't believe it! I couldn't even eat my welfare breakfast.

Wednesday night came and I'm shaking in my boots, sitting in the pulpit looking out over the audience at thousands of people. Bishop Blake had never heard me preach and I was ready. While I was in the house for about a week after dealing with the Andraé Crouch situation, the Lord started ministering to me through a song called *Press Toward the Mark*. The Word says *we have all sinned and have come short of His glory, but we can learn from our own mistakes.* One thing we've got to do is put the past behind us and press toward the mark. God used those words to encourage me and, needless to say, that's what I preached about. Press toward the mark! The power of God anointed me that night and I delivered myself. That's really what happened. The congregation responded in a powerful way like I had never experienced in my life. A few days later, I got a phone call from Bishop Blake's secretary saying that Bishop wants to meet with me. I went and met with him and had an opportunity to talk to him about Bishop Benjamin Crouch as well as Andraé and Sandra Crouch. I shared all the things that transpired between us, and he just sat there and listened attentively. He didn't say anything and what I admire about him to this day is that he never said anything negative about them. He said to me, *"We learn from our past, but I believe God has a great future for you and hopefully here at West Angeles. You can learn and grow and get involved in ministry."* What a difference in the two men, but he also said, *"I'd like to bring you on staff."* He put me in charge of the Tabernacle Choir, and eventually I would become Assistant Director of Social Services. He relocated us from almost one hundred miles away to about fifteen minutes from the church. Wow!

West Angeles became my place of growth development, and Bishop Blake became the father I never had. I watched how he treated his wife and how he treated people. I had an opportunity to travel certain places with him and to see how he handles various situations. I even had an opportunity to look behind the curtain, and found there was no difference between him being backstage and on stage. He was the same godly man. The crazy thing about it was he reminded me of my biological father.

He was tall just like him, he was eloquent just like him and spoke like him. I couldn't help but think about the promise God made. He said, *"I'm going to place men in your life who will father you."* Well, Bishop Benjamin Crouch was one, I'll give him that credit. He was, but not everybody is in your life to teach you what to do. Some people are put in your life to teach you what *not* to do. Now I'm not saying that it was all bad, as I did learn a lot from Bishop Benjamin Crouch, but I wouldn't be who I am today, the pastor, the preacher and the husband had God not placed Bishop Blake in my life.

West Angeles is where I got my start musically, and I give God praise for that. Later on I would meet Bishop G.E. Patterson of Memphis, Tennessee. He is in heaven now. I'll never forget the first time I preached at his church, Temple of Deliverance. After the service, I was in his office. He was so impressed, when I was ready to leave to go preach at another church, he called me back and said, *"Elder Hutchins come here please."* He was sitting at the end of his conference table. I went and stood beside him, and he told his adjutants, *"Leave us please."* They closed the door and now I'm standing beside one of the greatest giants in Christendom. At the time, he was the Presiding Bishop of the Churches of God in Christ. Now I'm standing there like a little Joshua star going into the eyes of a Moses. In that moment, Bishop G.E. Patterson poured into me. I mean I remember to this day many of the things he said. He said, *"Son, God has anointed you. You're gifted and you're talented. God is going to use you."* Then he began to caution me to not be like certain people. He named names I won't mention, but I will tell you one thing, they're no longer ministering. They've fallen from grace because of exposure and getting caught up in things. Apparently, he saw it coming and told me to be careful and to stay true to God. He even asked me, *"What are you doing musically?"* I said, *"Well, Bishop, I just finished recording a CD for JDI records and my wife and I were thinking about starting our own label."* He said, *"Well, why don't you sign with my label and do a record with me?"* Oh, my God! I said, *"Yes Bishop, I would love to!"* He said they would promote it through his Soul Winners conferences because he was doing them all over the country. Rance Allen was one of his favorite singers, and he would put me on there as well. I'm was like, *"Wow, I get to travel with G.E. Patterson and Rance Allen across this country at Bishop G.E. Patterson's Soul Winners conferences."* We start preparing to make the record, but he didn't make it three months before he died. I still have the contracts with his signature. So, as I stood on that porch in North Carolina, the Holy Ghost said to me, *"I'm going to place men in your life to mentor you and to father you."* What is so amazing to me is God went to the top of the Christendom totem pole and out of the darkness, out of the ashes, I emerged and got so close, I could see it, I could hear it, and I was a sponge. God placed me amongst Bishop Benjamin Crouch, Bishop Charles Edward Blake and Bishop G.E. Patterson. He gave me three for one. When my father forsook me, God became my Father. To think He became my Father through these three giants, and I am who I am today because of these three great men. Later on in life, God would connect me to other giants like Bishop Thomas Weeks, Sr., Bishop Liston Page II, and I mean the list just goes on and on. So God, I thank you for giving me what I need. Now God I submit to you. Show me some Joshuas that I can pour back into.

CHAPTER SIX

MEETING 31 SIBLINGS

There were many things about my family I didn't know, but as I got older, I began uncovering things that were both puzzling and shocking. As a small child I knew my mother had twelve children—Six boys and six girls. I was the baby boy. My sister, Velveteen, we call her Tiny, is my baby sister. I didn't know my siblings Pat and Elmer Lee had different fathers. I also never met or knew my brother Johnny who is deceased. It was puzzling that his last name was Phillips as my mom was married to James Hutchins. Some of our last names were Phillips, and some, the last name of Hutchins. I never gave it much thought. Even with my sister, Wanda Kay, to this day we don't know who her dad is. Even she isn't sure. Wanda looks mixed with something. I will say one thing, which my sisters will probably not like me for, but I think Wanda is the prettiest sister in our family. She is bright, business-minded and retired from her career at an early age.

I think about my sisters Faye Marie, Velveteen (aka Tiny), and my brothers Jimmy, Johnny, Michael and Tony. Everyone I just named has the last name, Hutchins, including me. The difference is they all had the same father, James Hutchins. My father was Earl Lee Garner, but my mother gave me her married last name, Hutchins. As mentioned in previous chapters, James Hutchins was an alcoholic ninety percent of the time. What I find so amazing is my older brother Jimmy, by about four or five years, had been an alcoholic most of his life and that is how he died. He drank so much that his liver was severely affected. Eventually Jimmy developed cancer and died. He was found in the house with his medicine and alcohol on the table. My brother Michael, who is just a few years older than me, has also been an alcoholic pretty much all of his life. Michael suffered a tragic life as a teenager. At eighteen years old, he and some of his friends apparently attempted to rob an old man and mercilessly beat him up. The old man was in the hospital for a week or so and eventually died. Michael and his friends were charged with murder. All I ever really remember about my brother is him being in a small, North Carolina prison, and my mother would take us to see him. I don't remember going inside the actual prison, but it seems we were able to see him by standing outside on the opposite side of the fence.

I believe there was a generational curse of alcoholism on all of my brothers whose father was James Hutchins. Even my brother Tom (his last name is Phillips and we're not sure who his dad is), died the same way my brother Johnny died. He was found in his bathroom dead from alcohol. We never even had a funeral for him. This was the same brother who served in Vietnam.

I was never close to any of my brothers. The only brothers I remember being at home when I was growing up are Jimmy and Michael. The rest of them were old enough to be on their own. I used to love it though because every few years my brother Elmo Lee, who lived in New York, would surprise us with a visit. He would always entertain me with the most interesting stories about how he used to protect himself and how he always had a gun with him. Each year he would bring me an instrument. One year it was a bass guitar that he showed me how to play. My goal was to learn how to play it so the next time he came home, he would be proud of me. Another year he brought me a saxophone that wasn't as easy to learn, but I did get the hang of it. Then yet another year he brought a keyboard and that was more like it! I used to write my little songs, and me and my sisters would all be in the living room. One morning, Elmo Lee came home and surprised us at 1:00 or 2:00 in the morning after being gone for two or three years. We talked all night long and enjoyed eating good food and singing. These were probably some of the happiest times I remember with family. Even back then I didn't know that Elmo Lee and I didn't have the same father. Later I learned his father lived in Virginia.

Throughout all this time, I had no idea I had twelve other siblings on my biological father's side, the pastor who passed away in 1991. I met some of my brothers and sisters on his side for the first time at his funeral. It was so confusing to me because, I looked more like them—on his side—than I did like anyone from my mother's side. Everybody on my dad's side was nice, but not to be played with. I think the most confusing thing was how they took a liking to me right away. I mean, I never felt that kind of love and support from the siblings on my mother's side like I did on my daddy's side. It wasn't reciprocal in the beginning because I didn't have the experience of growing up with them. Even after my biological father passed, his wife loved me as if I were her own son. In many ways, she reminded me of my mother. Interestingly, they had been best friends—my mom was the church pianist, and my dad's wife was, of course, the First Lady. Oh what a movie that would make! She embraced me, I'm telling you, and treated me very special. She was a cook! Lord, have mercy, could this woman cook! She's the reason why I love red velvet cake today! I would go visit for Christmas and, sometimes Thanksgiving, and they would have a spread that was out of this world! All of them treated me like they were there when I was born. I mean I'd never felt that kind of love. They knew I was a recording artist, were really proud of me and absolutely my biggest fans and supporters. It was nothing for us to be out and about and they introduce me to folks, *"Hey, I want you to meet my brother! Meet my brother, he's a recording artist! Have you heard this song called Scatter Blessing? That's my brother!"* Sometimes I would be so embarrassed, but I guess that was just their way of demonstrating how much they loved and appreciated me. I just hope and pray they felt from me what I was feeling from them, because sometimes I just didn't know how to express how I felt about them. I never really had that type of closeness, even from my siblings on my mother's side. My mom had twelve children, my biological father and his wife had twelve, and I'm one of seven out of wedlock. That's thirty-one total. I'm the only preacher out of all of the boys.

I suffered the worst treatment from two of my brothers from James Hutchins' side of the family and both were alcoholics. I was in North Carolina and my brother Johnny who drove an 18-wheeler truck said, *"Norman, come go with me."* He was going from Kingston to a place called Washington DC or Wilmington, I can't remember which one. He was sober when we left Kingston, but it seemed every twenty or thirty miles he would stop, pull over and get something to drink. By the time we got where we were going, I knew my brother was drunk. I had never seen a drunk man drive a truck the way he did. It was unbelievable he could still drive that big truck, but I was so afraid. When I got back, I didn't want to go anywhere else with him and he cussed me out. Lord knows he did.

Jimmy, the brother I really didn't care about, treated me really badly. He would hit me for no reason and looked just like James, the stepfather who abused me. I thank God I was never sexually abused. Looking back over my life, there were times when men said inappropriate things to me, or times I intuitively knew something wasn't right. At nine or ten years old, I just had this thing inside my gut that guided me away from it all.

We were poor, too, so many times we really didn't have a lot of food. There was one time when we had no food in the house. It was during summertime and Jimmy had cooked a big old pot of rice. He miscalculated or mis-measured how much rice to use, so the pot filled all the way to the top with rice like it was popcorn. That's all the food we had in the house besides some bread. I was begging for some rice because I was so hungry! I'm like, *"Jimmy, can I please have some?"* He said, *"No, kid,"* then pushed me away. You know what I'm saying? I'm standing over to the side crying and whimpering, and kept on asking. He got up and walked away. When I turned around to walk away, I'll never forget it. He kicked me so hard in my behind I flew up in the air like a football. When I came down, I couldn't breathe for I don't know how many seconds. God knows I could not breathe. Jimmy had knocked the breath out of me. How could my own blood brother treat me so bad? The truth of the matter is I found refuge in my friends. They treated me better than my brothers growing up. I never really had major relationships with my sisters because they were just busy at life and in their own world, especially when they became teenagers. It was boyfriend time!

Now, my sister Ree, her real name is Marie Ethel, would take me to kindergarten. Mom was busy working in the fields with tobacco. She drove a truck around the community picking up workers. So, she was always working. Ree took me to my first day of kindergarten. She was like Mama. Even to this day she looks just like mom. I'm sitting there in kindergarten, and she's over there on the side. I'm playing with some toys or whatever. I start thinking, *Now, I know she ain't trying to leave.* When my sister got ready to leave and started walking towards the door, I screamed to high heaven! She couldn't leave. She stayed. My sister stayed with me the whole day. As a matter of fact, I don't remember how many days passed before I was able to stay by myself. I was so afraid. I hadn't been around kids like that, and this was during the 60s when there were no White kids and no White teachers. All of the schools were segregated at that time. I was a scary little kid, scared of everybody. When it came to singing, acting and entertaining people, oh my gosh, I was bold and brave. That's what I was born to do.

My oldest sister on my daddy's side is Mamie Jay. Let me tell you about Mamie Jay. If you want to get in trouble, mess with me. I don't even understand how she had taken such a liking to me. She is from the country, too, and calls me Little Boy! If I'm anywhere near North Carolina singing or preaching, Mamie Jay's gonna be there. She loves her little brother. She'd say, *"My little brother, big boy! Looking just like Earl Lee Garner," talking about our dad.* She told me one time, and I believe her too, "*I was there when our daddy made you.*" She explained that when she was a little girl, about nine years old, she remembers our dad used to come to my momma's house. He would tell her he was going inside to pray and told her to stay inside the car until he came back. Mamie Jay said by the time he came back to the car it was dark and she had fallen asleep. He got in the car, and I guess went home. That must have been some serious prayer. I love Mamie Jay and don't tell her often enough. Actually, I love all of my sisters on my dad's side. Now, Lord have mercy, I have a niece we call Lucky Cary Carter. She could actually be my sister and not my niece. I love her so much, and she is probably the prettiest young lady on my dad's side. She is a pastor now and I am so proud of her. You can tell she has my dad's blood in her because, like myself, we are both just charismatic preachers, it's in us. Yeah, and I have twin brothers I've only seen in photographs but never met. I was told they were really bad, always into stuff, and don't believe they are alive today. I can't imagine what it would have been like to have known them and if we would have been close enough to create a pack together. Then there is my brother Jermaine. We are almost the same age, and my wife says he looks just like me, only a little bigger and buffer than I am. I used to be but not anymore. He's married with a family. I don't think he, of course, is not a preacher or anything, but I remember we were there a few years ago for a funeral for one of my sisters named Train on my dad's side. She was the crazy one with a mouth for days, but she was sweet as she could be. All of them could cook. I remember once he was at the house after the funeral and I just stared at him from a distance. He looked like him. We could have been best friends; I really believe that because even when we talked to each other, we were just so cordial. It was like we automatically had so much in common.

One of the things I've learned from all of this is that our sin doesn't just affect us, but it affects people that are connected to us. It has a domino effect, affecting the lives of so many people because of our selfishness and not being disciplined. Even when we do make mistakes, not making the right choices to do the right things. I was going down there for three years preaching at his church and didn't know he was my dad. Somebody could have told me. How can you grow up having twelve brothers and sisters and not know? I have another sister who has the same dad, but she has a different mom. Her name is Hilda, and she lives in Jacksonville, North Carolina. She used to own a soul food restaurant called Hilda's and, let me tell you, that woman knows she could cook. It seems like everybody always went to Hilda's. She fell in love with me, too. One day she said, *"Look at you, you look just like me."* Well, I don't look back with regret. What I do is thank and praise God I did not repeat the sin of my father. Sometimes people say the apple doesn't fall far from the tree, but that is not the case here. I've been able to look at the mistakes of other people and decide that I don't want to live that way. It's not that I'm better than anyone else, it's that life is about choices. When you make good choices, you get good results. When you make bad choices, you reap a harvest you may not want.

At the end of the day, I love my family. I think I want to do better in terms of building a relationship. I have a sister named Angie. I believe we are the exact same age, but she looks just like her mom, my dad's wife. What I don't like is it seemed Angie and I should have been close. She's respectful to me, and I'm respectful to her. We just didn't grow up together. Every once in a while, she'll reach out to me and I'll reach out to her, but the closeness is not there. How can you have thirty-one brothers and sisters and not feel close to any one of them?

My Career and Music

As I began pursuing life, my career and my music, God began to elevate and bless me. I moved to a whole different level. Some may get upset from me saying this, but it's my testimony. I had to say to my family, *"If I'm gonna be your brother, it shouldn't cost me."* Just because I worked hard, have a career, and my music is doing very well, being played all across the country and the world, and there are benefits that come with that. I was doing my best to meet everybody's needs and help them financially, but it just got to a point where I had to make a decision. *If I'm going to be your brother, it can't cost me financially.* When I did that, everything changed. I paid one of my sister's rent for one whole year. After the year was up, she said, *"Well, can you pay a certain amount continuously?"* I would pay car notes for a whole year, you know, things like that. One of my brothers asked, *"Can you can you lend me $12,000 to buy a truck?"* I asked him, *"I've been helping you with your house now, how can you pay me back?"* He said, *"Well, you got it."* That kind of stuff! Family can be worse than strangers. I guess the saying is true, it is lonely at the top. The higher God takes you, the smaller your circle gets. An old preacher taught me a lesson. He said, *"Always remember, the word 'no' does not need an explanation. No just means no."* You do not have to explain why you said no, and I was always used to doing that. No is a complete sentence and, when you learn that, you'll see how fast your circle becomes smaller. So, success becomes bittersweet. On one side you're excited because the things you have dreamed about, the things you have prayed about, you are now living and experiencing. You never thought it would cost you your family and even your friends.

My God, but I thank God for my wife. She is my best friend and has made so many sacrifices for me, it could fill a book all by itself. She's not selfish, loves me unconditionally, and has never done anything to hurt me. We are twenty-five years into marriage now. It's amazing what genuine true love between two people can do when there is an innate understanding of who we are and how God has brought us together. I thank God for my brothers and sisters and wish we had a better life together, but life moves forward not backwards. What I never wanted to do is pretend. No one has to pretend. You do not have to feel what you do not feel. Love and respect is all in life I ask you to give to everybody. There is nothing more special than that. Just love and respect.

Growing up in a large family can be like a roller coaster, up and down. What I mean is everything wasn't bad. There were good days and bad days, good months and bad months, good years and bad years. One thing

I didn't realize, as a small child growing up in a big family, is how poor we were. Big families have a way of making life work, especially living in the 60s and growing up in the 70s. Things were so different. It seems that the things you couldn't afford were simply lived without, and you managed just fine without ever missing them. I think about the young kids today. Some things we had, but how we had to live and adjust to life would be so strange to them. Like something as simple as water. A child can go in the kitchen, walk up to the refrigerator, take their glass, put it under the dispenser, and get crushed ice. Then get crystal-clear water from the same dispenser and drink it just like that. But growing up as a child, our water came from an outdoor pump. Some call it a well, and you had to pump it with your hand up and down. A bucket was placed under it to capture the water, but there's a thing called priming the pump. If you did not know how to do that, you never got water. You take a cup of water and while pumping the pump, pour the water into the top, and somehow that water connects with the water in the well. That's when crystal clear water comes straight out of the ground that is already cold.

Let's talk about the telephone. Children today only know about the cell phone. Back in my day, we had a rotary dial telephone. I saw an experiment with modern-day children between six and eight years old. A rotary phone was placed in front of them, and they were asked what it was. None of them had a clue; they had no idea what it was. It's amazing how life has changed.

Growing up as a large family during special holidays and Christmas, we enjoyed without all of the things that go along with them. We couldn't afford a Christmas tree, so we went out in the woods and cut down a pine tree. We made our own bulbs and everything, so there was never a sense of being poor. I remember one of our favorite dinners I always looked forward to. I didn't know it was considered the poorest of the poor dinners because I didn't know we were poor. My mother would get some self-rising flour, mix it with water and create biscuits. Then she would get a slab of bacon, cut it up into strips, put that in the oven, then get a jar of molasses. When it was time for dinner we had hot biscuits, molasses and strips of bacon. That whole meal probably cost about $5.00 because the bacon actually came from my grandmother. Every year my grandma would kill a couple hogs. She always had hogs, and we used to watch my grandfather kill them. My goodness, they cut that thing up and we'd have bacon and ham. They ate everything from that hog, from the router to the tutor. I used to feel sorry for those hogs. I guess that was the little preacher in me. I knew their day was coming when my grandfather would take the .22 rifle and shoot them right between their eyes. He would go up to them with a big knife and cut them under their shoulder so they could bleed. Then they were hung by their hind legs so the blood would drip into a basin. The preacher in me had to go preach to them and pray for them the day before their assassination, or the day before they went to meet their Maker. I guess that was the compassionate young preacher I would later become.

Many times, my grandmother would say to me or some of my other brothers, *"Go get me two chickens."* Now when she said go get two chickens, she wasn't talking about going down to the market. She meant for you to go out in the yard. Poor chicken...he's been minding his own business, walking around just enjoying himself. Grandma meant for us to grab that chicken by his neck and ring it. You would wind it up like you were twirling a yo-yo and then once you twirl it and it gets tight, you pop it. That chicken's head would come off and of course the preacher in me prayed for them. Before I would kill them, when their head would pop off, the chickens would jump around on the ground until they died. We always clapped our hands and stomped our feet because it looked like they were shouting in church. Even though they were dying, we felt they were shouting their way into heaven. When they stopped moving, my grandmother had hot water waiting. She dumped them in the hot water and started plucking their feathers. Then she would cut the chickens open, gut them and slice them up. The end result was some of the best fried chicken you ever put in your mouth! I'll never forget. Sometimes when you killed a chicken you didn't realize it was in the process of developing eggs inside of its body. So, the chicken was cut open, you could see the eggs, but they hadn't yet developed their white hard shells. The full egg was in a clear sack with a visible yoke that was edible! If you think a white egg tastes good, oh a chicken egg in the sack before the chicken laid it tastes even better. Wow! My point is, growing up, we never really knew we were poor. My grandmother had her own garden. If you wanted collard greens, you go to the garden. You wanted green beans, go to the garden. If you wanted tomatoes, go to the garden. If you want potatoes, go to the garden. I thought this was normal for everyone. I didn't know people were going to the store buying frozen vegetables and storing them in their refrigerator freezer. I had no clue then, but those were the good old days. I call it, when food was real food. So much has changed. I remember my mother started training my sisters how to cook. I had a couple of them who couldn't get it right, but my sister Renee Marie got it right to this day and is the best cook in the family. She even looks just like momma. Her mannerisms sometimes are just scary. For Christmas and Thanksgiving she could cook a spread that would have you coming back for seconds and thirds and fourths and fifths! Growing up in the South, everybody had to have that *to go* plate. I think it is because life was so simple back then and we made do with what we had; you weren't so stressed out. You didn't worry about the Joneses because we had each other.

Life has changed so much. People are willing to commit suicide if they do not have the money to buy non necessities, things of pleasure. We were poor but life was simple, and we were grateful for everything we had. To this day, I have no idea how my mother who passed at fifty-four could be a single mother of twelve children after her divorce. I know how hard it was with only three, but she made it work. She did the best she could. When I think about it, all I see is her coming and going, coming and going. She would work here, work there, church here, church there. Because she was a musician she played and sang at different churches. We didn't go with her many places because of her busy schedule, and as the girls were getting older my mom made them take care of the younger kids. Doris Hutchins, if you were alive today, your baby boy would say to you, *"I'm proud of you mom. I had no idea the things you've suffered, the things that you've endured, the things you hid from us to protect us, and even when you had men who you were interested in dating. When they would try to touch my sisters, you got rid of them. You never let them come back to the house. I wish I could remember more details about you, but I know you loved every one of your children personally and individually. You understood everybody's personality."*

Something was always going on in our house. I mean *always* going on! My brother coming home drunk, smoking a cigarette, and the house catching on fire. Jimmy is in jail and she had to go get him out. I remember when one of my sisters got pregnant, I was the first one she told, and I ran straight to them. I'm sure she was upset with me. I have another sister, my oldest, who is in heaven now. I remember when she used to live in Kentucky and was living with this guy. Her circumstance was very abusive. Similar to the way my mother dealt with her own situation. I'll never forget the day my mom got in the car with a couple of other people. She was driving to Kentucky to get my older sister who I hadn't seen in years. Her name was Shirley. When Shirley got home, we were all so glad to see her. She shared some of the things she suffered and went through with us that are inappropriate for me to include in this book. All I can say is God was with her. So, yeah, growing up in a large family is like a rollercoaster ride. Good days, bad days, ups and downs. When you add it all up, it is your past pain, past failure, past defeats, and also past victories that has prepared you for life.

A Gifted Family

We were a gifted talented family; I mean everybody sang. My sister Shirley played the piano at different churches just like my mother. My brother Johnny played piano, and my brother Emil played drums and bass guitar. When I started preaching at eight years old, my mother took me up and down the East Coast, preaching at different churches. We became known as the Hutchins Family. My sister Faye, mom and I were known as the Hutchins Family. We would always sing before I preached. There were some places we would go where we were just on a singing program. That's what they called it back then. They invite you to their singing program. The only music we had was my mom on the piano. We stood near her as she played and led a lot of the songs. One of the songs I used to lead was called *Somebody's Calling On Him All The Time.* I must have been about nine or ten years old leading that song. We became quite popular! Back then there weren't recording CDs or cassettes, only 8-track tapes. One lady suggested we record an 8-track tape. So, one day while we were singing at church, someone recorded us and I did just that! It sounded so good to hear my mom on the piano. She reminded me of Shirley Caesar. She had that kind of voice. In other words, my mom could sing and preach at the same time. That's how I learned.

We had really high hopes as a family in terms of becoming known across the country and perhaps even recording. As life moved on, we got older, and everybody started having their own personal drama. My sisters became teenagers and became so distracted with boys that when it was time to sing, they were nowhere to be found. As mentioned before, when my sister Ree got pregnant, I was the one she told. She made me promise not to tell mom, but she said it before she told me though. When she did, I thought about us not being able to sing because my mom was a straight holy woman. Pentecostal! Sure enough, my mom wouldn't let me sing anymore and fake not being pregnant. It got to a point where it was just me and mom. I never thought how it made my mother feel, or even what her hopes and dreams were for us. Did she desire that we have a career singing? Was that her plan? I don't know what my mother's dreams were in terms of music, but what I do know it made her happy when she played a piano and see her singing with her. I remember mom saying to me as we were on our way traveling, *"It's just you and me now, Norman."* I always wanted to please her, never to disappoint her. I didn't like the look on her face when she was upset or disappointed, so we started traveling. My sisters were busy raising their children and getting involved in promiscuity while experimenting with drugs and alcohol. Life can take you down pathways that can alter your destiny. I was likewise exposed, but I thank God for His protection and that I never had the same desire.

Music was so embedded in me and kept me focused to not experiment with a lot of things young people were doing. Even as a teenager, I was always afraid of *that* life. I was afraid of going to a club, I was afraid of getting drunk, I was afraid of all that. I believe my mom appreciated my preaching out of the fear of God hitting me. Nothing was more precious than to see me and my mom in front of hundreds of people. I'm standing next to the piano she's playing, and we're singing two-part harmony. There was a group called the O'Neal Twins, twin brothers that used to sing. One of them played and they also always sang two-part harmony. I think we kind of patterned ourselves after them. Mom would teach me songs she wrote but there's only one that I remember. I'll have to record it one day. It was bittersweet because I missed my sister singing with us. People were being blessed. I had no idea that one day it would all come to an end. My God, mom, why did you have to get sick? My mother would get sick, go in her room and stay there for two, three and maybe four days. Then she'd come out and was good to go. We were back at it, but when she went in the room this last time, it was different.

It had to be destined for me to be a preacher, singer, songwriter and producer. I've been doing this now for over thirty-six years. It's been my life because as a child it consumed me. I'll tell you something funny. I used to take the picnic table in the backyard and create a stage. I would get all the lawn chairs and my neighbors assembled in front of it. My friends in the neighborhood were good at gymnastics and could flip and roll almost as good as circus performers. I was always afraid to jump and flip because I thought I would break my neck, so I created what I call a variety show. I invited my mom, my sisters, the neighbors and everybody! They would come, chill out in the chairs, and I'd get on that picnic table. One by one my friends would come out and they would flip. They could flip backwards, I couldn't, but I could flip frontwards. Next, I would have them get on their knees, like three or four people in a row and I'd run, jump and flip over all of them. They would clap and start flipping backwards, frontwards and making all kinds of amateur gymnastic moves to entertain ourselves. Then I would sing and of course you know, hey I was a Michael Jackson fan and could sing every one of his songs, *ABC, I Want You Back*, you name it! I could dance too, Lord knows I could dance, just like Michael Jackson. Truth be told, I wanted to be an entertainer, but I was a church boy. Somehow, on stage I incorporated what I learned in church with my favorite artist, Michael Jackson, and it was just unbelievable! What I didn't realize at the time was I would one day grow into what I'd always done. Now the crowds are not just sitting in lawn chairs in my backyard, but they are in arenas, concert halls and parks, and not just here in America, but around the world.

Sometimes you become what you pretended to be in childhood. My family always pursued jobs to pay bills, eat, and live. As they grew up and got older, they moved out, but I always chased my dream. Always!

What drove me was a strong desire to do exactly what I'm doing now. When I was young I wrote so many songs, but only remember one of them called *Behold The Lamb.* You could tell I wasn't a mature writer at the time but as an adult, my songs are birthed out of life experiences. As a child I hadn't lived long enough, but boy now have I got a testimony in my songs. My God yes, I do!

I don't remember if any of my brothers or sisters graduated from high school. I actually went to college and, out of thirty-one brothers and sisters, I'm the only one who graduated from theological seminary. I earned a master's degree in counseling and hold a doctorate in church administration. No one else in my family has achieved that status and to ask me how I did it without an example, I couldn't tell you. It seems there are always two trains of thought that follow you through life. The thought to do right and the thought to do wrong. The thought to pursue good and the thought to pursue bad. The zeal and desire to make what you were dreaming a reality, and the desire to just keep on dreaming. I think one of the things that helped me, and I know this was God-given; nobody did this but God. He made me a daydreamer. Oh, was I daydreamer! I could just sit, and in my mind be so far away. I would daydream about different things that I would be doing in places I would be and people I would meet. Looking back on it now, I think sometimes my daydreaming was a band-aid for my pain.

Like some of the things I experienced growing up; feeling neglected, abused and abandoned. How can you be in a family of thirty-one brothers and sisters and yet still feel abandoned? I can think of at least five siblings in my family who thought it was nothing to slap me upside the head, punch me or whatever. I was ornery, too, and always mischievous and into stuff. One of the worst things is when somebody bought my mother a toy car. It was an older model car with a shot glasses on the side of it, like liquor glasses. The container in the middle was empty and I guess that's where you would put the liquor. Music would play when you pick it up and I would sing along to that familiar old drunken song, *"How dry I am, how dry I am,"* which means you need to refill it. My baby sister had a doll baby that had a motor in it, and it would play a certain song, like a nursery rhyme. Now I don't know how I got this idea, or even why I did it, but I took the motor out of my mother's toy car and put it in my baby sister's doll baby. Then I took the motor out of the doll baby and put it into the car and put it back on the shelf. One day my mom was showing some of her friends the gift somebody had bought her, and she told them, *"Listen."* Well, she picked that thing up and instead of it playing *how dry I am,* it played my baby sister's music. Now this lets you know how ornery I was, she knew how to call out the kids who did it. I was the first one she called! *"Norman! Come here. Did you do this?"* You know I wouldn't go and lie to Mama. No, that's something you don't do. She could read right through me. I said, *"Yes, ma'am."* She didn't whoop me then, but she made me put it back. Yeah I was ornery then; compassionate sometimes in my orneriness if that's what we can call it.

I remember when my baby sister wet the bed and I overheard mom tell her she was gonna whoop her for doing it. Mom had to leave to go to the store and she was on the come back, so I said, *"Don't worry I got you, I got you."* So, I put about four pair of pants on her. She was tiny and must have been about seven or eight years old. I put about four pair of pants and five shirts on her. I mean I padded her good. I said, *"Now when Mama comes home and she starts whooping you, just start crying and screaming."* She said, *"Okay."* When mama came home a little later, she called Tiny and said, *"I told you I was going to whip you didn't I?"* Mama went and got her belt and started whipping Tiny and this girl wasn't crying, she wasn't jumping, she wasn't screaming. Tiny just stood there like she couldn't feel it. When Mama checked her out and saw all those clothes on her she said, *"Who did this?"* My sister said, *"Norman did it,"* and so the beating that she got, quite naturally I also got. Yes, I was ornery growing up so it wasn't always their fault.

Some of the punishments I got were from my sisters and brothers. One time my sister Ree left the iron on. I guess she had to iron some clothes, left the iron on and fell asleep in the room. I walked in there and saw that the iron was plugged up and still warm. This girl could have burned this house down so I called myself gonna teach her a lesson. I took the iron and held it over her hand. I wasn't going to touch the back of her hand. I was just gonna let her feel the heat and then wake her up and say, *"Girl, look what you did, you almost burned this house down!"* but as I was holding it over the back of her hand the iron got heavy and that dag gone thing messed around and touched the back of her hand. When she jumped up and saw what I had done, she beat me like a bass drum. Do you hear me? I mean she beat me so bad until I got on my bicycle and rode from Georgetown to Bridgeville where my grandmother lived. That must have been about fifteen miles. Can you picture a young kid on a bike riding fifteen miles? But, that's how bad it was. I was so ornery. Wow!

My older sister Shirley is in heaven now. Apparently, she was pregnant with her son Ronnie at the same time my mother was pregnant with me, so we grew up together. I thought he was my brother, not my nephew until I was almost an adult. So, Ronnie, my nephew, my sisters Wanda, Velveteen (aka Tiny) and I spent a lot of time together growing up and playing because we were very close in age. I think about what kinds of toys poor children play with when some parents can't afford to buy the popular ones that some my schoolmates had. Well, because of my imagination we created our toys! Yes, we did! I would take an old tire from an abandoned car and get behind it and just roll it. In my mind, it was a bus because I was fascinated by school buses. I would pretend it was a bus and, every so often, stop and pick up children and take them to school. I could play that role all day. And, oh, a broom! I would take a broom and straddle that broom pretending it was a stallion horse. I would gallop all around the yard.

We also had this game we used to play sometimes until 3:00 in the morning. We called it Money! I guess an adult might have called it Economics. The way the game worked was we all had to keep running. We all had a different spot in the living room that we considered our house. We would decorate it; I mean we'd have momma's stuff all over the place making it our little house. Now, because of my imagination, I was the bank and the boss man because I owned the business. I had a restaurant and a workplace and was also the pastor of the church. Next, I took paper, and I cut it into small pieces to make money. They called it paper money and I put numbers on it like $1, $5, $10, $20. My sisters and my brother worked for me because, of course, I had to be the boss. Their job was stuffing envelopes. That was amazing to me because that's actually a job. So, I had stacks of paper on one side and envelopes on the other side and they would fold the papers and stuff their envelopes. I don't know what we were sending out in the mail but anyway, time playing those games went by fast. After five minutes or so, the whistle would blow and they would be finished working. Then I ran over to my little restaurant and take a piece of toast, cut up the toast, with cheese and just find anything in the house I could use as my menu. They got paid on Friday. My workers could come to my restaurant and have to order food. I would pay them with a check and they would go to my little bank. I would cash their checks and give them money. The money would then come to my restaurant and we repeated it all over again. It was like a circle. Then there was the entertainment! We put on a little show and they had to pay for that, too. Everybody had something to do. It was like I was the Mayor of the town and owned all the businesses. I owned the bank and everything. We would play that game sometimes until the sun came up in the morning.

They Called Me The Mayor

Years later, as an adult, you could walk down Main Street in Dover, Delaware and find my six businesses. One of them was a restaurant called The

Lunchbox, another was a music store and then I had a shoe store called Shoe Fashion. I also had a jewelry store called Jewelry Mart and another business called Just Jeans. My wife Karen had a clothing store called Karen's High Fashions. Not to mention, I also owned the Private Party Room too! People were calling me the "mayor of the city." Then of course I was a pastor with a church right up the street on Frontline.

One day I was walking downtown from business to business checking on them when, all of a sudden, I had this thought in my mind. I was doing the very same thing as a kid that I was doing as an adult. As kids, we were playing with play money, but now, as an adult, I'm doing Economics. I was creating jobs for people in the community I was always meant to be the leader, a businessman and an entrepreneur. The craziest thing about it, nobody told me my father disowned me. I didn't grow up with him and my stepdad abused me. None of my brothers and sisters were business-minded, and most of them dropped out of high school. So where did this come from? How did I pursue it? Well, I can only say one thing, it was God. The Bible says, *"(God) He shall give you the desires of your heart."* That scripture really means He will give you something to desire. When I was born, everything I am today was already inside of me, but it was in seed form. Anything God gives you comes in seed form. As you grow in life, it will grow as you make right choices and right decisions. Someone said, *"If you ask God for an oak tree, He will give you an acorn because the oak tree is inside of it."* Your job is to plant it, cultivate it, and allow it to produce. That's the way life has been for me. One of the things I learned about myself growing up is I never spent a lot of time mourning and grieving over loss and things that didn't work right for me. I made the best out of a bad situation. I don't know where I got that from, but it was always in me. I was never the kind of person to prove people wrong. No, because I always felt like the underdog anyway. I always felt like I didn't deserve this, and I didn't deserve that. I always felt like everyone else was better off than I was. So, for me, just being normal or not exceeding above others just felt normal. I felt like I had to do double the work, especially when I didn't know how to read, write or even do math.

Speaking of math and reading, my grandmother was just like Mama to us. She could whoop us and whatever, but she couldn't read or write either. I'll tell you what, my grandmother bought a brand new Buick every two to three years, and she didn't want it off the lot. She wanted it from the window. I mean it had to come out of the glass because they heard it was brand new. If it was on the lot, that was used. She never knew how to read, she never knew how to write, and she never had a driver's license, but she always had a brand new Buick. I remember one time she bought this Buick. Back then we called the model a *Deuce and a Quarter*. It was a beautiful, pretty green. She would ask mom to drive her to the store or the bank and the feed store to get food for her hogs. And, boy, when I got old enough to get my driver's license and started driving grandma around, it felt like her car was my car. She never drove. So, sometimes, once we got home, she would let me drive to the store or the mall or wherever, and I'd come right back. Wow, she couldn't count, but you couldn't cheat her out of her money. I don't know what kind of accounting system my grandma put in place. I promise you, if she gave you money to go to the store to get something, when you came back, she could tell if she had the right amount of money. I don't understand it to this day. She used to keep her money wrapped up in a handkerchief hiding it in her bosom.

I guess I'm saying all of that to say I was the same way. I couldn't read or write, but I was dreaming about business entrepreneurship. I think the first barrier to success you will ever have to overcome is believing in yourself. In my mind, you'll never be successful at life doing anything, if you do not cross that barrier. I have to believe I can! How can a young man who doesn't know how to read or write? How dare you dream of owning a restaurant, how dare you dream of owning six businesses downtown, but life has a way you know. What I've learned is everybody has the ability to learn, it's just that everybody doesn't learn the same way. Do you understand that there's no difference between you and the next person? You have to learn at your level. You have to learn at your pace! When I read today and when I do business today, it was always in me. It was just going to take a little more time for the light bulb to come on for me to say, *"Oh, I got it now."* The tree, that is you, is in the process of growing and developing at your own pace. Others will perceive you just don't get it—you're dumb or there's something wrong with you. How can you be this age and not know? Are you telling me you are in high school and cannot read, you can't write? Oh, something must be wrong with you. You know, I think I survived it all because the voices in my dreams were louder. Oh man, that ministered to me just now! The voices of my dreams were louder in my head! I didn't know how I was going to get there or how I would learn, but I thank God! I think the Holy Spirit, Father and Son must have gotten together in the boardroom of glory and said, *"Okay, what are we going to do about Norman, because here's what we've already predestined for his future—to be a pastor, a doctor of theology, a singer-songwriter, and a producer. We want him to reach back and chronicle the Bible from Genesis to Revelation. We want him to graduate from theological seminary with a doctorate in church administration and a master's in biblical counseling. How do we get him there with no teachers?"* I guess they must have all agreed, *"Let's do two things. We will give him the gift of memorization and we will help him along the way."* I'm telling you, those two special gifts brought me to this place where I am today, and I'm grateful to God. I don't even understand sometimes how my sisters survived because I know many of them experienced the same thing in school. I remember one of my sisters dropped out of school in the 12th grade, and I can tell, even to this day she struggles.

"My God, but Father as I look back over my life, all I can say is You were there all the time. I do remember one time in my life I said to You, 'I thought I was Your child. I thought I was special to You. I thought You loved me,' because things seemed like they weren't coming together. Then I remember You telling me through the Holy Spirit, You said, 'Norman, you're complaining about what you're going through, but you're not thanking Me for what you have survived.'" My God, I apologized and repented of that because the truth of the matter is you can't have sun without rain. No! There will be sunny days, and there will be cloudy days, but all of it is designed to make you grow. I think one of the major keys to life is not just understanding who you are and what your purpose in life is. But, always turn back to the Manufacturer, the One who created and made you and say Thank You. I thank God wisdom and time has brought me to this place where I'm now able to understand everything that I went through. Everything I've learned has brought me to this place today. I guess that's the reason why I'm doing my best to document my life. So when I die, I die empty. That is my desire. I want every dream and every vision, I've ever received from God, to come to fruition before I go to heaven. I want my life to be just as effective when I'm gone as it was when I was alive so, perhaps, I can help somebody. Maybe not to avoid your pain, trouble, trial or adversity, but maybe I can help bring some understanding to why you must go through what you've got to go through.

I think about the life of Joseph, one of my favorite Bible characters. Joseph was hated by his brothers and sold as a slave. He was thrown in a pit and lied on by Potiphar's wife. He was thrown into prison. He didn't ask for any of that. That was what life gave him, but in every season of his life he excelled and emerged to the top. So, it's not what life gives you, it's about what you do with what life gives you. When Joseph was promoted to second in command of the Pharaoh's Kingdom, he was able to institute a program that would sustain them through a major famine. Eventually, when word got back to his father and his brothers that Egypt was the place where they could survive, Joseph recognized his brothers before they recognized him. He sent for his baby brother, Benjamin, and his father. Then invited his brothers to the table, and they dined with him. When they recognized it was their brother, Joseph, they feared for their lives. They knew he remembered what they had done to him, and he had the power to command their lives. But Joseph looked at his brothers and said, *"What you meant for evil God meant for my good."* This is one way you know you're ready for your elevation in life. When everyone who has produced pain, caused you pain, have not treated you fairly, and when you are able to have the spirit of Joseph and say,*"What you meant for evil God made it for my good."* If you cannot say that, you're not ready for elevation. Because when you're elevated to a place of power where you can affect people, that could be dangerous. It's going to be through your humility and forgiveness that God ushers you into your purpose and into your destiny. One of the greatest miracles of my life is that with thirty-one brothers and sisters, the greatest miracle in the midst of all of that is God always had His hand on my life. Out of the ashes pain from my past, God has allowed me to become a voice in the Kingdom, and for this I'm grateful. If I can just help somebody as I pass through, then my living will not be in vain.

It's not about what life gives you, it's about what you do with the life you've been given.

CHAPTER SEVEN

STANDING BY HIS GRAVESITE

Standing by the graveside of my biological father, who disowned me as a child, wondering what could have been and what should happen can cause bitterness and resentment. But, because I chose to forgive a dead man, my past was buried with him, and now I am free to embrace my future. I refuse to live in the past because the past has no value. The past will never propel or launch you into your future. Forgiveness is the key. Forgiveness unlocks the prison cell of your mind and your emotions. It frees you to explore life and to pursue your purpose and destiny. One thing is for sure, I will not go backwards. The apostle Paul said, *"Forgetting those things which are behind and reaching for those things which are before I press toward the mark for the prize of the high calling of God in Christ Jesus."*

As you begin to grow in life, one difficult challenge you will face is not knowing who you were. I think not knowing the foundation of your path sometimes tends to affect your future in a negative way. There are things you will do, things you will desire and you're not able to connect it to the reason why. It is so important that children be nurtured in the environment of a healthy family, where you can actually see the roles. What is a mother? What is a father? What is the responsibility of a father to the wife and to the children? What is the responsibility of a wife to the husband and to the children? What are life's do's and don'ts? How does a child process life without a guide, without navigation, without the love and nurturing of parents? Well, one thing I have learned is, if you do not have it, life will give it to you. You will gravitate toward people you will emulate and glean from. They become your portrait of life. The blessing is if you are committed to Christ, He will put the right people in your life who will teach you values.

One of the tragic end results of many young people in the world today is not having the example of what a real father looks like during childhood. For me, as a child, the example of a father was alcoholism and physical and verbal abuse against women—particularly a wife. After my mother divorced her husband, there were only about three other men I remember coming around during my mother's lifetime. Watching them, I never saw an example of what a father should be. They were never married to my mother, were never in the home full-time, and would just come and go. As a child, I really didn't understand it as relational or sexual. That's all these men were interested in. I think it really takes a different kind of man to want to commit and marry a woman who has twelve children. Because my mother was so vulnerable and looking for love in all of the wrong places, she gravitated to the wrong kind of men who only came around because they had a hidden agenda.

I must have been about twelve years old; I remember this one man whose name I can't remember. We started seeing him off and on. He must have felt, in order to get close to my mother, he needed to get close to the children. One day he asked me if I wanted a pony. I'm like, *"You mean like a horse pony?"* He said, *"Yes, but it's not a horse, it's a pony. That means it's smaller."* Well, you know he had my heart, of course you know it doesn't take much for a child. I remember the day he unloaded the pony off the back of his truck and as soon as I saw him, I named him Billy. My pony Billy! I built a shack for him in the backyard. My mom's suitor told me how to take care of him, and Billy became my friend. At night I would stare out of my bedroom window to make sure he was okay, and I played with him every day. The only problem I had with Billy was he would never let me ride him. Every time I got on his back and tried to ride him, he would bend that long neck back and try to bite my leg. I would jump off every time I tried to ride him. When I saw my mother's friend, I told him, *"Billy will not let me ride him."* He said, *"You can't ride him when he's eating. He has to stop eating before you can ride."* I said, *"But he eats all the time."* He replied, *"Well, once he gets full, he'll stop eating and then you can ride him."* I'm telling you every time I attempted to ride Billy, he was always eating so I came up with an interesting idea. The key was to ride him so he would not turn around and try to bite my leg. I remember looking at the Kentucky Derby on television. Now that I had a pony I was interested in horse racing, watching them race and all that goes with it. I noticed the men riding their horses weren't on theirs backs. They were on a little two-wheel carriage with the long stems that strapped across the horse's back, then tied and looped from the top of the horse around his belly. A bit was put in the horse's mouth with long ropes making the horses rideable. I went and found some wheels, plywood, and two by fours. I don't know where I found that stuff, you know, somewhere in the neighborhood where I grew up. There was always junk around that we used to make things from. As children we didn't buy toys, we made our toys. I made this carriage, and wrapped it around Billy, tied it tight and sat in the back. In place of a whip like the pros had, I found a long switch. I got in back of the carriage, folded my legs and held on. I took my stick whip and hit him on the back of his behind, *"Go Billy! Come on let's go!"* Let me tell you, he took off running down the road and I mean he was running! All of a sudden it dawned on me, I had nothing in his mouth, I had no way to control the direction he would go! How could I have forgotten the bit for the horse's mouth? I started telling him to, *"Stop, whoa, stop. STOP!"* The more I said stop, the faster he ran, and now what was supposed to be enjoyable is one of the most frightening moments of my life. *"Stop, Billy, stop!"* I'm holding on for my dear life, and he was running down the road. People were looking and laughing. I think what happened was he decided to go to the left, down this dirt road. Billy made a quick turn, that carriage broke off of his back and I went tumbling. I mean I fell. I scraped up my knees and my elbows. Thank God nothing other than that happened. Finally, Billy came to a stop. I guess he was telling me, *"You will not ride me. That is not why God created me. I'm sorry!"*

Every Young Boy Needs An Example

So finally, I got Billy back home. I was upset with him because he wouldn't let me ride him, but he was still my best friend. I took care of him and would at least lead him around with a rope around his neck. He would follow me, but never let me ride him. I was left to enjoy taking care of him by washing and feeding him. When winter came, I wished I could bring him inside because it was so cold. He looked like he was freezing when snow fell, but when Spring rolled around, Billy was happy. Then one day, without explanation, my mom's friend took him. I lost my friend and didn't know why! Why would he give me a pony and then take him away? As a child, I didn't understand that it wasn't because I couldn't take care of him. Now that I'm older and looking back, I believe my pony was connected, he really was. He was connected to my mother. I know this because their relationship didn't work out, and he took everything he brought into the relationship including Billy. Standing at the graveside, I was wondering who would now become the example of a man in my life. How do I grow to become a strong black man? Some of these things can be so puzzling when you're a child. Every young boy needs that example. If you don't get one, life will teach you and, oftentimes, it doesn't teach you the proper way.

When my wife and I first got married, during our first two years, I noticed I had symptoms from my experience with negative men I had seen growing up. Like the way I responded to conflict and the way I felt a man should treat a wife. I was never physically abusive, but I learned later in life that verbal abuse is just as bad as physical abuse. I thank God, one day the Holy Spirit began to minister to me about repeating the cycles of negative men who may have influenced me. He told me I had a choice, but I refused to go down that road. I do not like where it ends. Standing by the graveside of my father wondering, *"Will I be like you? How much of you is in* me?" Life teaches you that you do not have to be the person you witnessed growing up. You can choose. It is your decision! You are not under a family curse. Just because your father was an alcoholic doesn't mean you have to be one. Just because your father was abusive to his wife doesn't mean you have to be. Just because your father did not take care of his children doesn't mean you shouldn't. You have a choice to do the right or wrong thing. But when you're standing by the graveside of your father whom you didn't know, what you do know are the stories of his past, his frailties, his shortcomings, his sins and, you know, the things he did that he shouldn't have done. Bury it with him. You should not allow his past to become your reality. So, I chose not to be a graveyard digger. I will not. I refuse to take up the emotions of my father. I refuse to dig up the sins of his past. I refuse to become the things he was. That is not my purpose, my destiny, nor my future. Now after being married for twenty-five years to the most beautiful woman in the world and, looking back on my past, presently I can say I have broken the generational curse of my father. I am not what the grave says I am. I will not be what the grave says I should be because God has placed powerful men in my life. I will emulate them. I will learn from them. I will be the man that God has created me to be, and that's my legacy. I will teach other young men, whose example of a father is only the grave.

Forgiveness

Let's talk about the power of forgiveness because that's really where it all starts. Standing at the graveside of my father, I was doing a lot of thinking. I have thirty-one brothers and sisters, many whom I didn't know till later in life. I was preaching at my biological father's church, who was a pastor of two wonderful churches, and didn't know you were my father. I was walking down the hallway, then standing next to you when someone asked you who I was. You denied me as your son, and then you died. I have so many questions that will never be answered, yet I decided at your gravesite to forgive you for not owning me as your son. I must admit at sixty-two years young today, when I talk about it and when I think about it, it's disappointing but not painful anymore. It is like a scar that has healed with no pain, but the scab is there. I know why, because I made a decision to forgive. The thing about forgiveness is it doesn't release your offender; it releases you so that you do not imprison yourself for the rest of your life. So that you do not blame yourself for what happened in your past.When I meet and I talk with people today about forgiveness and they begin to share their story with me, it almost seems like they want to justify their choice not to forgive. They add up all of the things a person may have done or even said to them as if they are trying to convince you to choose their side. You have every right not to forgive that person for what they did or what they said. At the end of the day, it is your choice. Well, what you will learn is that in not forgiving people, you"e not forgiving yourself to move on. It then shows up in your work, your relationships, how you do business, how you treat people and, God forbid, if it was relational, marriage. It hinders you from giving another person the opportunity to experience the totality of who you are. You're always holding back life in reserve, anticipating that what happened to you from someone else will happen to you in your present and in your future. You're not always free to live. That's what forgiveness does. It frees you to live. The older you get the more you look back over your past, and you're grateful you did. Otherwise, it will cost your life, it will cost you relationships, it will cost you friends because, without saying it, you really will not trust people at a level of freedom. Forgiveness allows you to trust people at a level of freedom. Free to be happy, free to walk in peace, free to live! That is powerful to me and that's why I was able to move on. I broke the shackles off of me. This is a biblical principle. Even Jesus says forgive and it shall be forgiven you. Then He also goes on to teach us that if you do not forgive men their trespasses neither will your Father in heaven forgive you your trespasses. No wonder life is so bogged down and does not produce a harvest. It's because the principle of forgiveness is not being practiced. Forgiveness breaks chains; it opens the prison door so you're able to live. When a person chooses not to forgive, they cheat themselves out of so much. When I stand and preach today through the freedom of forgiveness, I am able to talk about the challenges of my life, my past, and things I've experienced; particularly my father, and not feel the pain that was associated with it. I look at it as life lessons. What do you do when life presents challenges and situations you did not create? You choose not to allow it to imprison you. You treat it as a step ladder to the next season of your life to move on and move forward. What I've learned over the years is, the further away you get from that date of whatever happened, happened, whatever you discovered, the further away you get from the date. Particularly, if you have forgiven that person. Mark the date. Mark the day you forgave the person and the further away you get from it. The more it dissipates. The more you feel better, the more we are able to move on with life and get to a point where you can talk about it without negative feelings. I've learned about forgiveness. You know when you have forgiven someone. You can talk about it and not feel the pain. If you talk about it and still fill pain and it brings up all kinds of emotions, bitterness, resentment, and anxiety; you obviously haven"t truly forgiven that person. When you truly forgive a person, at some point you can talk about things and not feel the pain associated with it. What I'm really trying to say is, your pain turns to gratitude. If you do cry and get emotional, it"s not because you're feeling the freshness of the pain of the disappointment. Now you're walking with a spirit of gratitude, thanking and praising God. What happened to you did not take you out, it did not destroy you! You did not lose your mind great God today! You made a decision, *"I will move on, I will live choose to live!"* My brother, choose to live! My sister, that's what I've done. That's what Im doing and now my only desire in life is to in some small way, encourage you, inspire you, and push you over the cliff of forgiveness so you can soar and become productive. One thing I've learned about walking with God. He will not prosper you if you're walking and living in unforgiveness because hurt people hurt people. God prospering a person with unforgiveness can be dangerous. When you have the authority and the power to get even, you may not always use it for good reasons. Forgiveness has a lot to do with where God takes you and how you allow him to use you to help bring an end to someone else's pain. That's it.

The Aftereffects

One of the things people never think about while they are indulging in things that can be detrimental to their own lives is the aftereffects.

In my case it was my biological father who was married at the time and having an affair with my mother. What he didn't consider is how mistakes or sin would affect the lives of others. I am a result of sin. I am a secret that nobody wants to talk about. I am fleshly, selfish, and private. My biological father took pleasure with someone and did not take into account what would happen if my mother got pregnant. Who would take care of the child? How would he grow up? These things were not taken into consideration. My mother was pregnant with me, and they kept it a secret. I was born without a choice. I didn't get to choose who my mother would be, nor who my father would be. I didn't get to choose the circumstances around my birth or to grow up as a child who was lied on. No one told the truth about who I really was. As I grew up, things told to me were later discovered to be false. Circumstances like this can affect your true identity, your self-esteem and overall being. The questions you eventually begin to ask is, *"Who am I? Why was I born? Why me?"* Life has a way of exposing the truth. I've learned that when the truth is exposed, even though you were born in a situation like I was, without a choice, when you become older you do have a choice! You have the choice to make decisions that can affect you in a negative way for the rest of your life, or you can take the life you were given and make it work. You can become productive and successful because the one thing no one can take from you are the gifts the talents God has predestined for your life.

It is so interesting to me that I have been a preacher now for the last fifty-four years. Also interesting is that I am a gospel recording artist and have been for the last thirty-five years. I have two Grammy Awards, one gold and one platinum album. I have recorded fifteen CDs, and my music is played on the radio and heard around the world. I saw a video of mine that had thirty-million views! Just one video, and I have hundreds of videos on YouTube and other social media platforms! What I'm trying to say is, I inherited being a preacher from my dad and I inherited music from my mother. My dad was the preacher, and my mom was the piano player and singer. So, God took both gifts, wrapped them up into one and gave it to me. There was a drive inside of me that I cannot explain. It's like I knew what I had to do. That was my life's call. When I was working at McDonald's mopping the floors in Delaware, I knew my future was bigger. When I was cleaning the trash at homes, I knew my life was bigger than that. Every job I ever had helped me to survive and sustain myself and my family. Yet, I knew there was much more. One thing I've learned is, when you focus on pursuing purpose and destiny, you do not have time to make pit stops to dwell on your past. Not only will stopping distract you, it will slow you down. The truth of the matter is, I've had multiple opportunities to allow my past to bring me to a halt. But back in 1991, I recorded a song on *Saints In Praise Volume II* through West Angeles Church of God in Christ and Bishop Charles E. Blake as the pastor. The title of the song is *Let's Press Toward The Mark*, which I believe God gave me to be the fuel I would need to not dwell on the past, but to move toward my future.

Another lesson I learned is to turn your pain into power! Yes, turn your pain into power, and press on toward the mark for the prize of the high calling of God in Christ Jesus. When God has a calling on your life He uses everything you have ever experienced and gone through to ultimately become your testimony. So, when I was standing at the gravesite of my father with hundreds of questions in my mind, knowing he would never have the ability to answer, I knew one thing. I refused to get in the grave with him, so I released him and I forgave him. When they buried him, my unforgiveness was buried as well. At the end of the day, the date will end. When you wake up in the morning, you wake up with the freshness of sunshine and unlimited possibilities that are not restricted by the pain of unforgiveness. You are ready to receive and accept the wonderful possibilities that today just may be the day something great, something good is going to happen. Like when I was recording with *Saints In Praise.* I did three songs on the record that night of the live recording. After the recording we went to the studio to do some overdubs. Just a small portion of the choir and the owner of the record company, Mr. Billy Ray Hearn, who is no longer with us, was there to listen to his investment. He was the president and founder of Sparrow Records in Nashville, Tennessee. I will never forget how he pulled me to the side in the drum room, shut the door and asked me, *"Do you have any more songs like that?"* I said, *"Yes sir!"* He had no idea the list of songs I had written prior to meeting him. Many of them were songs birthed out of the pain of not knowing my father, and of me forgiving him and moving on. So, when I said, *"Yes sir,"* in that drum room, he said, *"I would like to sign you as a recording artist on Sparrow Records."* I could not believe what I just heard! People dream of this for years. Mr. Billy Ray Hearn gave me a five-year contract. I've recorded two albums with Sparrow Records, and that music is still being played and heard to this day. So, when you wake up every morning, you wake up with new possibilities.

God doesn't bless people standing still. He blesses people in motion. So, you have a choice. You can either sit still and rehearse the pain of your past or you can move forward. I think about David, one of my favorite Bible characters. He and his men had gone out of the city and when they came back, the city Ziglag was burned down. I mean it was burned down to the ground. Even their wives and children were taken captive. So, David and his men, as tradition would have it, began to mourn with sackcloth and ashes. That was a historical practice. Sackcloth was like goat skin, typically dark in color, that they would put over themselves. Then they would take things and burn it to make ashes. They would then take the ashes and sprinkle them on their heads, and sometimes even sit in the ashes. All of this was symbolic or an outward expression of their inward feelings of grief and sorrow. They were lost, but what caught my attention when I read this story is when the Bible said David grieved seven days. Hmmm, why not ten days, why not thirty, why not a year, why not five years? It specifically says David grieved seven days and, after the seventh day, the Bible says he inquired of the Lord. *"Should I pursue after the Amalekites?"* and the Lord said to him, *"Pursue and in your pursuit, you will recover all."* When I read that, the revelation I got from it was, it's okay to grieve over a loss. It is okay to grieve when you experience things like being disowned by your father and not having someone there. I never had anybody at a basketball game or football game or even to go with me to the movies, and it's okay. David grieved for seven days, you see, because the only way you're going to pursue, you have to take off the sackcloth, brush off the ashes and start pursuing.

I said to myself, *"You've grieved long enough."* Many people grieve beyond seven days, and it's okay. The problem is, at some point, you have got to take off the sackcloth, brush off the ashes, and pursue life. Yes! Pursue it! Go after it! When I look back over the last thirty-six years of my life in music, fifty-four years of preaching and sixty-two years of living, I pursued. I can't say I remember what day it was or what month it was or what year it was, but at some point I do know I took off the sackcloth, I brushed off the ashes, and I am where I am today. We give glory to God our Father.

CHAPTER EIGHT

ABANDONED BY LIFE

"He Never Knew I Knew"

After my grandmother revealed the secret that the alcoholic, James Hutchins, who I thought was my biological father really wasn't. She also revealed the pastor of the church where I had been preaching for three years in a row was actually my biological father. This really answered some of the questions I had. I always wondered why the pastor cried when I would come and preach. No other pastor cried the way he did. He would hug and grab me, but never mentioned I was his son. It took my grandmother to disclose this information. Now that I knew, I waited for the opportunity to let him know I knew, or hope he would mention it to me. Growing up in the 60s as children, you never were allowed to ask grown-ups questions. That's the way we were raised. You don't get to ask them questions. You hope they will answer them along the way. Walking down the hallway of the church, on my way to the sanctuary to preach, he was confronted by one of the mothers of the church. She asked him, *"Is this your son?"* I heard him say, *"No, mother, this is an evangelist from Delaware."* At that moment, not only did I feel abandoned, but I felt like nobody wanted me. How can this man be a pastor of two churches, have me out of wedlock with my mother, but more than that, leave me to be raised by a man who knew I wasn't his son?

I used to wonder why my stepfather treated me the way he did, but as an adult, of course, now I know. He was always in and out of jail. During the time he was in jail, apparently, my mother and the pastor had an affair, and then I came along. Because he abandoned me, and did not own me, I was raised by a man who did not like me, was an alcoholic and knew I was not his. He was abusive to my mother and abusive to me. I could always tell when he was really upset and mad at my mom because I received the same treatment, probably sometimes even worse. I remember being afraid of him, especially when he was drunk. I would do my best to stay out of sight. Oh, if something was missing, I was blamed for it. If he was mad about anything he would call my name, *"Norman!"* and hit me with anything in sight. A broomstick, extension cord and sometimes with his bare hand. There were times he was abusing me, and no one even knew. Not sexually, but physically so I used to stay out of sight.

One of the things I used to do in Kingston, North Carolina was go up under the house and play. I was so small I could almost stand up. There was nothing but dirt under the house so that was always my safe place. I would go play and could stay under that house for hours and hours, sometimes until it turned dark. I would take some of my little toys, like my taco trucks and cars, and create roads. One of the games I played I had no idea was not only a game, but it was also prophetic. I call it playing with the toys of my future. What I would do is take a cigarette box, turn it upside down and pretend it was a stage. Then I would get rocks and put them on top of the box and pretend the rocks were a choir singing. I would get one nice rock, put it out front, and that was me directing the choir and singing. For hours I could just pretend I was traveling all around the world with my choir. Then one time I went and got a couple of egg cartons, you know the one with twelve slots, and put rocks in each one of them. I'd get about two or three more of them and pretend they were buses. Busloads of people coming to my concerts. I would dump them in front of the cigar box stage and pretend I had a packed audience just listening to music. Fast forward years later, now I am the minister of music at West Angeles Church pastored by Bishop Charles E. Blake. I am the Director of Social Services and also the State Minister of Music, over two hundred fifty churches.

Wrote a Song for the Olympics

One day two White gentlemen came to my office and said they were referred to me.They were looking for someone to write a song for a special event. They hadn't told me what the event was, but did give me the concept of the song. As they were talking, the melody and the words just came to me. The gentlemen liked it and said, *"We would like for you to teach this song to a 1,000 voice multicultural choir from around the world."* I asked what the occasion was, and they said it was for lighting the torch at the Olympic festival. I'm thinking, *"Did he just say the Olympics?"* Then he said, *"We need you to print up your sheet music so you can teach it to the choir."* Now we have a problem because I cannot read music. Everything I've ever done was by ear, but I'm not afraid of a challenge. So, the last thing I was going to do is tell them I do not know how to read music. I didn't want to miss this opportunity so I said, *"Yes sir!"* I went to one of the sisters in my choir who knew how to read music and told her about this song. I needed her to put it on sheet music for me and explained that I had to teach it. She did just that. Next, I asked if she would show me how to sight read. She did her best even though all the notes looked like a foreign language, but I wasn't afraid of the challenge.

So, here I am at this big beautiful Catholic Church in Los Angeles off of Wilshire Blvd. One thousand voices are in the audience, H.B. Barnum, a mega name in music, is sitting at the baby grand piano teaching his song to the choir. I'm watching him read his sheet music, turning the pages as everyone is following along. Another gentleman gets up and goes to the piano with his sheet music. He sits there and begins to teach his music and does the same thing as Mr. Barnum. *"Mr. Hutchins, it is your turn,"* I heard the voice say. I am so nervous, shaking in my boots, yet unafraid of the challenge. I sat down at the baby grand piano, opened my sheet music on top of the grid like I knew what I was doing and said, *"Okay, everybody, let's turn to page one."* Because I knew the song by ear, I could play it, plus I wrote it. The choir sang along with me, and the only way I knew when it was time to turn the page is when I heard everybody else's page turn. Then all of a sudden somebody raised their hand and asked a musical question that I couldn't answer because they were referring to some of the notes on the sheet. *"Should we sing this note, that half note or the quarter note?"* My response to them was, *"What do you think we should do?"* They said, *"Well, I think we should sing the half note."* I said, *"Well, let's do that."* So, then we moved on about a couple more minutes, and someone else raised their hand with another question. Another hand was raised after that and I'm thinking to myself, *"Oh my goodness, these people are getting ready to find out I cannot read music."* Clapping my hands I said, *"Okay everybody, OK, OK, OK, OK, OK listen. Put your sheet music down. I want to show you how we teach music in the African American church."* I started singing each part, alto, tenor and soprano, then had them repeat after me. The choir learned the song within twenty minutes. I got up from the piano and closed my sheet music. As I was walking past the other gentlemen, I overheard them saying, *"How did he do that? Wow, that was amazing!"* To this day they never knew I couldn't read a note.

The climax is the actual event. Now I am at Dodger Stadium in Los Angeles standing on the director's box with my white gloves and my baton, still unable to read a note with a one-thousand voice choir in front of me. All of a sudden, the intro begins, and we start to sing the song I had written. Muhammad Ali, who was the reigning champ at the time I believe, was jogging into the stadium with the torch in his hand while I was directing the song. He goes up and lights the torch. Halfway through the song, the Holy Spirit tapped me on my shoulder and said, *"What does this remind you of?"* Well, for the first time in my life I saw that cigar box and those rocks under the house. When all I wanted to do was hide from an alcoholic so he wouldn't beat me, I didn't realize I was playing with the with the toys of my future. Everything I had imagined was now a reality. I was standing there, the stadium is packed to capacity, Olympic athletes from all around the world covered the ceiling to the floor until you couldn't see the grass. There were so many people and, again, President Ronald Reagan steps to the podium and gives a speech. This little country boy who couldn't read or write, who was in Special Ed from 7th grade to 12th grade, who was disowned by his father and abused by a man who thought was his dad, is now standing on a box with white gloves, baton and can't read a note. That has fueled me for the rest of my life. Not to ever be afraid to pursue something even though I may not qualify because the truth of the matter is people will only know what you tell them. Thank God for making my cigar box and my rocks a reality. No matter who you are, where you're from, your ethnicity, or how you were born, the fact that you're here indicates you have some cigar boxes and rocks, too, that no one can stop you from making a reality. The only person that can keep you from becoming the best version of yourself is you. I was told a story about a man who heard that there was gold in the hills.

So, he went and got a shovel and started digging in the hot sun. People teased him as they passed by and said, "*This man thinks that there's gold in the hills,*" and, all of a sudden, he got discouraged. Not because of what the people said, but because of what he started thinking in his own mind. So, he threw the shovel down and walked away. Another man who had read the same report went up the same hill, picked up the same shovel, dug one time and struck gold. The man who walked away did not realize all he had to do was dig one more time. You can't stop digging, you can't stop pursuing, you can't stop dreaming! You've got to pursue! That has been my life's story. I look at a challenge as an opportunity to pursue. You will never conquer anything if you do not try. A winner never quits, and a quitter never wins. You cannot become a victim of your past no matter how bad it has been. Every year there are new leaves on the tree. Every year, continue to pursue. Go to your cigar box and your rocks.

I'm here in Europe, Downtown Norway, in the lobby of this gorgeous five-star hotel looking at the beautiful ships as they come and go, thinking, I could live here if only I knew the language. I do not like to live in places where people can understand me, but I can't understand them. In many ways it reminds me of the 1960s during segregation. I woke up in the morning and went to go for breakfast. No one speaks to me, and I'm such an outgoing person. I like to speak to everybody, "*Good morning, good morning!*" no responses. They are rude. They walk in front of you and don't say excuse me. Not to mention, when you are at, let's say, a buffet, they reach over you, stand next to you, and don't even say excuse me. Wow! In many ways it reminds me of the 60s, yet it is a beautiful country.

This chapter is about being abandoned by life. As I think about that and how one overcomes thoughts of knowing your own biological father disowned you. I'm sure he had his own reasons for doing so because what he did was definitely not right, but why should I have to pay the price as well. Sometimes I wonder if he is the one who I got my drive from and where I got that thing inside of me that causes me to pursue life against the odds. Do I have his DNA of going after life? Or I don't know if that's just the way that I am. I remember living in Los Angeles after I first moved to California back in the early 80s. An old friend of mine had a job at a place called Advance Business Forms in Fontana.

One Day I'll Record at Capitol Records

I was working in the warehouse driving the forklift. My job was to load up the trucks from the pallets of stationary envelopes for the different companies who purchased them. I would always let my coworkers hear my music. I'd bring a demo to work and a cassette player say, *"Hey, you guys, check this out,"* and they would just love it! *"Man, you're good! We love your music!"* One day somebody said, *"Norman look!"* It was a few boxes on their way to Capitol Records in Hollywood. Jokingly they said to me, *"You should put one of your cassettes inside one of these boxes that's going to Capitol Records and maybe somebody will discover it and give you a call!"* I remember saying to them, *"Man I won't have to do that! I'm gonna record at Capitol Records one day!"* When I said that, I'm telling you, they laughed at me, and that became the warehouse joke. Yeah, the warehouse joke, because I was dreaming from the warehouse. Every day a box would come through and it had the name Capitol Records on it, even if I was way in the back of the warehouse somebody would scream, *"Norman, Capitol Records!"* I would just totally ignore them. Whenever I came around with my forklift, I picked up that pallet of boxes, maybe stationery or letterhead. Whatever it was, I put it on the back of the truck headed to Capitol Records week after week, month after month. I knew somebody was going to say, *"Capitol Records!"* and I just totally ignored them.

Fast forward to1991. I recorded *Press Toward The Mark* on Saints in Praise with West Angeles Church of God in Christ. That song took off, it really did. The owner of Sparrow Records, Billy Ray Hearn, offered me a contract and asked me where I wanted to record the album. I said, *"How about Capitol Records?"* The next thing I knew, I was standing in Studio A at Capitol Records, the studio Nat King Cole made famous. Now I'm standing there with a live band and a choir. We created seats for one hundred people as the audience so it could be live. The night of the recording I'm hearing the music and watching the people clap their hands and respond with their amens and hallelujahs. I'm thinking to myself, this is the same place where several years ago my coworker said I should put a cassette in one of the boxes, and I told them I would not have to. I had no idea what I spoke had now become a reality. Once the CD was completed, and the release date had arrived, I put a box of CDs in the car and drove back to Fontana. My warehouse coworkers were still there and hadn't seen me in about six or seven years. I put on a nice clean suit, too. I carried the box of CDs on my arm, and when I walked in the warehouse everyone was really glad to see me. I gave each one of them a CD, and they were so congratulatory. "*Wow! Wow! Wow! This is so nice. You finally did it, man! You did it!*" I said, "*Yeah, but turn over the CD, look on the back and see where I recorded it.*" When they saw Capitol Records, my God, that was a full circle moment, which reminds me of the scripture that says, "*Death and life are in the power of the tongue, and those who love it shall eat the fruit thereof.*" You gotta see it, you gotta speak it, before it is manifested.

I still had one order of business to take care of in Fontana. When I used to work in the warehouse, I wasn't making enough money to take care of a wife and three children. From time to time, I would go to the pawn shop and pawn one of my keyboards out of my studio. It got so they expected me at least once a month. They knew me so well until I didn't have to fill out new paperwork. At the time they would just give me $80.00 to pawn my keyboard. When I got paid, I'd come back and pay them, get my keyboard back and keep right on writing my music. I remember telling them one day, "*I'm going to come back to this pawn shop and I'm not gonna pawn anything. I'm going to buy something.*" You know how people can be, "*Yeah, Yeah, okay yeah. You've been pawning all this time, what makes you think life is going to change for you?*" So, I went to the pawn shop and they hadn't seen me in several years, just like my coworkers in the warehouse. When I walked in, they recognized me. I gave them a CD, too, and they were so excited for me! I saw the owner and said, "*Do you remember what I said to you?*" He vaguely remembered, but I reminded him and said, "*I told you that one day I'm gonna come to this pawn shop and I'm not going to pawn anything but I'm going to buy something.*" Then it became clear as a bell, he said, "*Oh yeah, you're right, I remember.*" I looked inside the jewelry case, and asked, "*How much is that ring right there?*" He told me the price, which was about $3,000 back then. I told him I wanted it and pulled out $3,000 cash. I paid for that ring I bought over thirty years ago and still wear it to this day. Even now, in this very moment, I call it breaking the spirit of poverty. Every time I look at this ring it reminds me when I had nothing, and now God has blessed us and prospered us. It keeps me humble. It reminds me that if it had not been for the Lord on my side, I wouldn't be who I am or have what I have today. So, this ring helps me to walk in humility. It teaches me to never walk in pride and to never discourage anybody else from dreaming like I did at that warehouse. You never know, your day at Capitol Records might be closer than you think. Did I get that from my father? I guess I'll never know. From the stories my older sisters on my dad's side used to tell me, it seems like I'm almost a replica of him in terms of my preaching, how I handle business and how serious I am when it comes to what I do. My oldest sister Mamie Jay says to me, *"You just like Daddy!"* That's the way she puts it. Mamie Jay is so country, she puts the "K" in country, but is just as sweet as she can be. I guess listening to her has given me more identity of who my dad was and probably anyone else I've ever known. She says he was eloquent like Bishop Charles Blake and poised like Martin Luther King, Jr. Even when I saw him and heard him speak, he did remind me of Bishop Blake and Martin Luther King, Jr., like two in one. I just wish I'd known him better.

Even when you feel abandoned, the thing that helps you pursue life is to make your dreams your best friend. Yeah, that's it! Make your dreams your best friend and go after them! I'm sitting here in the hotel lobby in Europe. These choirs are singing my music and I even heard them sing in their own language. I didn't know it by language, but I knew it by the melody they were singing my song. To think back now coming from a little country town in South Kingston, North Carolina where my father abandoned me, but my dreams gave me life. Right now I'm traveling the world encouraging and inspiring people through the music God has birthed through me. I am so grateful I cannot even find words to thank God for not allowing bitterness that could have been birthed out of abandonment to dominate my life. I was willing to forgive, and I was willing to make life adjustments and pursue. Everybody has a choice! No matter what life gives you, no matter your challenges or your circumstances, it's not what life gives you, but it's what do you do with the life that you've been given.

One of the definitions for the word abandoned is *"cease to support or look after someone."* When I think about that definition, it really sums up my life growing up as a young child, even into my teenage years. I always felt like I had no support. I felt abandoned. When I think back on it, I was in the school chorus singing the night of the concert at my school which would be my debut leading a song. I had no support, no family members, and no friends. When I was involved in a special club at school called VICA, which means Vocational Industrial Clubs of America, I entered a contest for extemporaneous speaking. The way it worked was you were given a topic on a small piece of paper and put in a room for five minutes with no paper or pen. You couldn't write notes, you had to study the topic, and you were allotted three minutes to speak extemporaneously. I came in first place at my high school, which gave me the opportunity to compete at the state level. I came in first place at the state level and then was nominated to go to the nationals in Atlanta, GA. This must have been back in 1976. I came in second place in the nationals only because of my extemporaneous speech. It was good and compelling, but I misunderstood one of the words in the subject.

Abandonment, A Dream Killer

My point is, at the local, state and national levels, I had no support. How can you have thirty-one brothers and sisters, not to mention all the cousins, nephews, and family members, and yet no support? That has been the story of my life. Even at my high school graduation, I had no support. I never really thought about it, but I guess that's just the way we were raised. Everybody was so busy living life and having their challenges, we were never taught to support one another. That's why it seems like I've always been so independent all my life. Even now I'm not sure if that's a good thing or bad thing, but one thing I do know is it built some resilience inside of me. I got to a place where I could look at myself in the mirror, and everything I wanted people to say to inspire or encourage me, I would say it to myself. I mean literally, I would speak it to myself in the mirror. I've always had that inside of me. No matter what I went after or what I was challenged by, I always gave it my all. Sometimes feeling abandoned, like no one cares, can become a dream killer. It can hinder your pursuit in life, but that wasn't me. I always reached deep down inside and found the means to move forward. I've always been a supporter of other people because I know how I wanted to be treated. I believe one of the keys to success and experiencing a successful career in whatever you do is never depend on people to be the support you need to get there. Sometimes you have to just row the boat by yourself. Through all the challenges that life will bring your way, you keep moving forward.

After I graduated from high school, I got a job at a restaurant called the Blue Gold Inn and I'll never forget it. I had completed two years of culinary training during high school. I would go to high school for half a day, and the vocation or high school the other half the day.

I had a niche for cooking. I loved to cook and became so interested when I got this job at the Blue Gold Inn. I started as the dishwasher and, no matter what I did, I always did the best I could. My goal was to have no waiter or waitress pile up my counter space with dirty dishes. You could come through that room and not see one dirty dish. I kept it clean. As a matter of fact, I was so thorough I had time to help the short order cook with his tickets. I was learning at the same time and did so well, when the short order cook quit, they offered me his spot. I went from being the dishwasher to the short order cook and, of course, I did the prepping as well. I prepped crab cakes, stuffed shrimp, steaks and pretty much everything on the menu. Now I'm the short order cook but I have my eyes on the head cook's position. His responsibility was to prepare all of the main dishes for the customers. I excelled as a short order cook so much so I had time to assist the main chef. For whatever reason, after about a year or so, he moved on, and I was promoted to head chef. Again, I excelled so much as the head chef, the waiters and waitresses started to get jealous because people in the restaurant would send tips to me. I would always get their orders right! Like medium rare steaks or a poached egg, I knew exactly how to prepare it! Everything was to their taste, and to show their appreciation, they would send me a tip. That was the story of my life. It always seemed like every time I excelled at something, there was always someone who was jealous.

One lesson I learned is you can't become what other people want you to be just to please them. You've got to maximize your potential. I was thinking about a parable the Holy Spirit gave me about a car. If your car, let's just say it's a Hyundai, and just for understanding this parable let's say your maximum speed is 20 MPH. No, I'll give you more than that. Let's say your maximum speed is 50 MPH. I mean pressing the pedal to the floor you're going 50 MPH. Now let's say I have a Jaguar, and my maximum speed, for the sake of the parable, is 80 MPH. I press the pedal to the floor doing 80 MPH. You press your pedal and you're doing 50 MPH But now here's the thing. I do not have the right to talk about you going 50 MPH. If 50 MPH is your maximum then you are maximizing your potential. If 80 MPH is my maximum, then I am maximizing my potential. All life requires is that you maximize your potential, but here's the other thing. If you're maximizing your potential at 50, why would you be jealous of me because I can go 80? We're both experiencing the same thing, maximizing our potential, simple as that. Now, let's say I decide I want to make you happy and please you. I don't want you to be upset with me or jealous of me. So, I decide instead of driving 80 MPH, I slow down and drive 50 MPH because you can only go 50. All right, so now you're happy you're my friend, but the problem is you are maximizing your potential but I'm not. I had to slow down to become equal with you. You're not encouraging me to maximize my potential, you're not telling me to go ahead because you are pleased. But, if I'm going to maximize my potential, this is what we may have to do. I'll drive 80 MPH, and you'll drive 50 MPH. I look over in the next lane and meet my new friends who are driving 80 MPH and you meet your friends who are driving 50 MPH. That's the key! It's maximizing your potential. Anyone who cannot keep up with who you are and where you are, leave them behind at 50. Matter of fact, they're so far behind you can't hear them anyway. I think that was a season of my life where I was not maximizing my potential. I was surrounded by other people who could not keep up. It is not your fault that you are gifted, talented and anointed. Sometimes you have to leave people where they are so you can go where life is taking you. They may feel abandoned by you, but that's okay because everybody can't go where life is taking you.

My dream and greatest desire growing up was to do what I'm doing today. I'm a songwriter, recording artist, singer, and preacher but, I tell you, nobody told me how hard it would be to get to this point. When I look back over the years of pursuing the dream I'm living today, I can say people see your glory, but they do not know your story.

One of the principles I've learned is success does not come without opposition, trial and adversity, and your dream has to be bigger than any trial you will face. I've also learned that you are guaranteed to fail if you stop trying. Your dream didn't defeat you, you really defeated yourself. Your destiny is always waiting for your arrival. If I knew years ago what I know now I could have avoided a lot of heartache and tears. The truth is, I think it is all a part of the process. I remember making a demo tape I gave to a radio personality at an event. They gladly received it and said they would play it on the radio. During that time, I didn't have a radio in the house, only in the car. Their show came on from 8:00 p.m. to midnight.

So, I would sit in the car and turn the radio on, hoping one evening to hear my song. Every time I listened, she never played it until after about six months. So, I started picking and choosing randomly when I would sit in the car. One night I was in the car after 10:00 p.m., fell asleep and had a dream. In this dream I was actually dreaming I could hear my song on the radio, and midway through the song I woke up. I could still hear the song, and it dawned on me, *"Wait a minute, she is actually playing it on the radio."* I remember that first night. It was between 10:00 p.m. and 11:00 p.m. I'm sitting in the car by myself. My song started and I heard my song on the radio and said to myself, *"If one station will play my music, I can't stop until radio stations all around the country are playing the songs God was giving me."* I can honestly say after thirty years of doing music, not only can my music be heard around the country on just about every major station there is, but now my music can be heard around the world in Europe, Africa, Japan, Spain and Brazil! All over the country and all around the world, wow! I was sitting in that car by myself night after night and the lesson is this, you cannot depend on people to water your dream, you've got to water it, cultivate, keep it alive in your spirit and keep moving in the direction of your dream. When you get discouraged, the Bible talks about how David encouraged himself in the Lord. You may have to do that sometimes.

When I hit rock bottom and what I mean by that is, I felt what I had been dreaming about and going after was not going to come to fruition. To make matters worse, I was at a concert and saw a national artist I really love. I won't mention the name because too many of you would know who this person is. I gave them a copy of one of my cassette tapes, which he gladly received. At the end of the event, as I was departing, I noticed my cassette tape was sitting on the table. I tell you, I was so discouraged. I remember later that week thinking, now not only am I not reaching my dream but I'm having financially challenges and trying to take care of a family. I know what I want to do and know what's in my heart to do, but it's not happening. I got so discouraged I took all my music equipment from my studio in the house, packed it up, and put it in the closet near the front door as you go out of the house. I told myself, *"This is it! I'm going to do something different. I'm not going to pursue music anymore because I'm tired of being disappointed. I'm tired of being hurt, I'm tired of being let down, and nobody's helping me."* That was my go-to—*nobody's helping me.*

So, every day I would leave the house as I passed by the closet where all my keyboards and recording equipment was stored.

One day I was driving down the I-10 freeway and saw this 18-wheeler truck with a big sign on the side of it that said Truck Driving School. I said, "*That's what I'll do! I'll go to truck driving school and learn how to drive an 18-Wheeler, and I'll just drive all across the country making deliveries.*" I will never forget it. I went to the school in Norwalk, CA and gave them my deposit. I got the application and while sitting at the desk filling it out, in my mind I saw myself throwing away my dreams. Not to mention the investment I'd already made for about fifteen years. I was so discouraged it didn't matter anymore. I wanted to do something different and didn't want to feel the pain of pursuing something that seemed like it was ever going to happen. Then something strange happened while I was sitting there filling out this application. Midway through it the Holy Spirit asked me a question. He said, "*What are you doing?*" I didn't respond and kept filling out the application. I heard him say it again, "*What are you doing?*" By this time, tears were falling from my eyes onto the application. The page was smeared by my tears, but I still didn't respond. He asked again, "*What are you doing?*" Out of my pain and frustration I said, "*You won't help me. I've been trying, I've been pursuing writing all these songs and being disappointed.*" I didn't think this either, I verbally spoke it. The Holy Spirit asked me another question, "*What are you gonna do when you're driving down the freeway in your 18-wheeler and you turn on the radio and hear a song that I meant for you?*" When he said that I tore up the paper and didn't even get my deposit back! I walked out and said, "*I just need you to help me God. Show me what to do.*"

One evening I went to a concert of one of my favorite 90s groups, The Winans—Marvin, Carvin, Michael and Ronald. They were singing a song that ministered to the pit of my soul. The line in the lyric that got me is, "*Are we really doing Your will we've come over a lot of mountains and all we see for miles are hills. I admit we get discouraged but that's just the way we feel I want to know are we doing Your will.*" I'm telling you that ministered so deeply to my soul. I became so inspired and encouraged I went home humming that melody in my spirit, opened up that closet door and pulled out my keyboards and my recording equipment. As I was putting it all back together, I got stuck on the phrase that says, "*I admit we get discouraged but that's just the way I feel I want to know are we doing Your will.*" I knew it wasn't the will of God to give up on my dream, but let me tell you something I did not know. One of the biggest songs of my career, *God's Got a Blessing With My Name on It* was in the closet. I have a Christmas song called *Emmanuel.* It is the most requested gospel Christmas song in history now next to Mariah Carey's *I'll be Home for Christmas.* I think that's the title, was in the closet. My first Grammy award-winning song *Jesus I Love You* was in the closet *Battlefield* was in the closet, *I Really Love You,* one of the biggest songs in the UK was in the closet, *God Is On The Way,* which was one of the favorite songs for the Scandinavians in Norway Europe was in the closet. If I had not gone back inside that closet and pulled out my dreams the world wouldn't know the songs God birthed through me.

What's in Your Closet?

I'm gonna pause right here just to ask somebody who is reading this right now. What have you put in the closet? What have you become so discouraged by that you put it down like me, feeling like it would never happen? The Bible says, *"The vision is for an appointed time it shall speak and not lie."* So, here's what I want you to do. I want you to get a book marker and put it on this page right now. Put it down, you'll come back to it when you finish. Now go and open your closet and, whatever you have put in there, get it out. Go get those plans you had, go get that book you were gonna write, go get the songs you were gonna sing, go get the business you were going to start. Whatever your dream was that you put in the closet, get it out, because what I've learned is that it is dark in the closet and isolation. Nothing can survive. You have got to get it out of you. You've got to birth it and spend the rest of your life pursuing. I'd rather die trying than to lay down, die and give up. Now when I look back after thirty-six years of doing music, having fifteen recorded CDs and I'm still doing music, it's amazing to me. Now I am in a position where I can help others musically by producing.

You know what else I learned about a dream? The fulfillment of a dream is just one door connected to many others. I'm doing things now that were not even a part of my dream. Because I pursued the dream, and the dream apparently had dreams, now I'm able to experience so many other things! Father, I thank You that I wasn't so discouraged and so disappointed that I didn't go back in the closet.

One of the questions I'm asked all the time is how do I get started in the music business and how do I make it a career? Well, the first thing I would say is, a boat is made for the water, which is to say you've got to get in the right environment. You should always surround yourself with the environment that will take you where you want to go and become a student of it. Learn from others. I was fortunate when I became a member of West Angeles Church, Patrick Henderson was the Minister of Music. I became part of the music ministry there and was blessed to become the director of the Tabernacle choir. During that time, we had five different choirs. I had the opportunity to teach my choir a lot of the songs I'd written. One of the songs was *Press Toward the Mark,* which became a favorite song at West Angeles. There were Sundays I would sing that song for all four services. The church itself had a recording contract with Sparrow Records out of Nashville, TN for the *Saints In Praise series* volumes one, two, three and four. When I joined, they had completed volume one. Two years later Patrick was beginning to collect music for volume two. Because *Press Toward The Mark* was such a favorite, everybody suggested to Patrick, the producer, to do that song and it almost didn't happen. He has so many songs but because everybody really pressed him, he decided to do it. Even so he didn't want me to sing the lead and had selected someone else. At the last minute, for whatever reason, the person couldn't do it. So, not only did I lead *Press Toward The Mark*, the song I'd written, but Bishop Blake had a favorite song I used to sing, "*Whose Report Will You Believe.*" Then Patrick had another song, *How Do I Say Thank You* that I ended up leading. So, the night of the live recording was a special moment. It was almost like I was a special guest or an artist, because I did three songs, almost back-to-back.

The owner of the record label was in the studio while we were doing the overdubs. He pulled me off to the side and said, "*We want to sign you to the label.*" That's how I got started! I surrounded myself with people who were doing what I wanted to do, and I learned, and I gleaned from them. When the opportunity presented itself, everything was already in place. One of my nuggets in life is, I'd rather be prepared for an opportunity that never happens than for an opportunity to happen, and I'm not prepared.

The other thing is you have to know your craft. I think one of the hardest things, sometimes for me as an artist, is to tell people who love to send me music to critique it for them. *You know that maybe this is not something you should be doing because the song lyrically doesn't really make sense, or vocally you're really, really challenged...* But I think I have so much compassion when it comes to that. I remember myself trying to get started. So usually what I do is, do my best not to give them false hope, but to share with them some areas where they need to improve. At the end of the day, you can have desire but not the gift to go with it. The Bible does teach us to covet. Covet the best gift! You just have to know what your gift is. Always remember this, you're not the only one with the same dream. If your dream is going to be significant, it's not that you have to stand out, but you definitely have to attract people who will love and appreciate what you do. So, there has to be something about it that's different from anybody else, and I believe that's how unique we are. The Bible says we are *"fearfully and wonderfully made,"* so there is a uniqueness about who you are and what you've been called to do. You just got to know it. You've got to know it, I'm telling you. With all the mountains and valleys you will have to overcome, you can't depend on other people to validate you, tell and remind you that, yes, you're gifted, you're talented, and you've got it. Before you step on stage, you got to know that in yourself.

I remember one time I was in Memphis, TN. This was after my second recording with Sparrow Records. I did a song called *You Were There* and back then in the 90s the midnight musicals at the Church of God in Christ National Convention had about eight to ten thousand people in attendance. I remember the night I was on the program to sing. Nobody knew who I was even though I was a new artist at Sparrow records. This was a promotional date, and I was sitting on stage next to the world-renowned Dr. Mattie Moss Clark, who is now deceased. She was the international minister of music for the Church of God in Christ music department. On the other side was Vanessa Bell Armstrong who was very popular during that time. So, I was sitting between Dr. Mattie Moss Clark and Vanessa Bell Armstrong on stage and group after group, singer after singer! BeBe and CeCe Winans, Richard Smallwood, I mean the list just goes on and on. I was waiting for my turn, and little did I know I would be the last person. It was probably almost 3:00 a.m., and when they called my name I walked out to the center stage. The track started and I began to sing my first line, which goes like this, *"Lord it was you when I was lost you came along and rescued me..."* By this time you would have thought somebody had given the benediction because while I was singing people were leaving by the hundreds. I became so discouraged I really wanted to just stop and walk off the stage, but I decided to close my eyes and said, *"God I'll sing this to you an audience of one."* The chorus of the song says, *"It's good to know that you were there beside me, it's good to know that you were there to catch my fall, it's good to know that you were there when I called, it's good to know that you are there."* At that moment it didn't matter that the building was now about seventy-five percent empty. Now we have more empty seats than people, but I had an audience of one. So, you've got to know who you are if this is the career you want. Not everybody's going to celebrate you, but you know what's really amazing? That same song, *You Were There,* was my second Grammy Award. Amazing, simply amazing! So, you just can't give up, and you have to know who you are. You have to study your craft and learn from others. I remember Dr. Mattie Moss Clark saying to me, *"You're gonna be alright baby. You're gonna be alright."* I wish she was alive today so I could say thank you to her because I'm alright now.

CHAPTER NINE

INCARCERATED BY HURT

"Do Not Let It Define You"

One of the things prison and hurt have in common are they both enable you to flow freely. They are confinement, limitations, and even isolation, but the difference between hurt and a prison is, hurt is like the invisible bars of a prison cell. It confines you, it limits you, and sometimes even produces fear of moving forward. It's kind of like drawing a line in the sand and you automatically know not to cross it. It's a funny thing what people will do when they experience real hurt. Sometimes we give ourselves a life sentence that keeps us from pursuing life, our dreams, purpose, and destiny. We want to avoid being hurt. Sometimes disappointment, failure, and defeat can be the root of hurt. The experience of pain from hurt can paralyze, but what I've learned is sometimes hurt can be ordained of God. What I mean is, not that God causes it, He doesn't prevent it. He knows and sees that going through those types of emotions and experiencing what real pain is all about can also be a part of maturing you, and helping you to grow physically, spiritually, mentally and emotionally. Whatever it takes to get you to the highest level of success is what it's going to take to keep you there. When I study the scriptures, particularly the New Testament, one of the greatest writers, the Apostle Paul, wrote many of his books from prison. What I find interesting is when you read some of his writings. It says in one text, *"I Paul a prisoner of the Lord,"* and in another text he says, *"I Paul a prisoner of Jesus."* It is interesting because the Romans imprisoned Paul, yet he never gave them credit for imprisoning him. He says I'm a prisoner of the Lord. Sometimes God will allow us to go through a season of incarceration where we are confined dealing with limitations.

On top of all that, having to deal with hurt and pain. Even though while we're going through it, it doesn't seem pleasant, and it certainly doesn't seem fair, it's needful. David, one of the writers of the book of Psalms says, *"It was good for me that I was afflicted,"* makes you wonder how can you glory in your afflictions? Well, I've learned that everything you suffer, everything you go through, all of the hurt, and all of the pain are part of developing your character and your outlook on life. It's like surviving the valleys of life before you can experience the mountain top. Gaining your blessings this way, you never forget where you came from, how God has exalted you and how He has lifted you up. One of my favorite scriptures is written by Apostle Paul. He talks about pain and suffering and said, *"The sufferings of this present time are not worthy to be compared with the glory that shall be revealed."* He teaches us that enduring your pain, your hurt, and your sufferings prepares you for the manifestation of glory. The blessing, the manifestation of the things you're going after, and that applies to every career, every dream.

No one is exempt from experiencing hurt and pain. Even a mother who will soon enjoy the pleasures of life when she holds a newborn baby in her arms. And, yet, before she can experience that, she will have to go through a season of pain. It is the birth canal; it is bringing something to fruition that no one else can help you birth. Dreams and visions are just like that. When God plants it inside of you, it is through your pain and suffering that is going to bring it to pass. You cannot let the incarceration of your heart define who you are. I am not what I am going through because this is just a portal, a highway we must travel. Everybody must come this way. What I've learned to do is tell my valley, *I'm not in a valley, I'm just changing mountains.* Anyone who has a mountaintop testimony will certainly have to have a valley testimony as well. It is the things you will have to endure that will prepare you for the challenges you will face at the next level of success. I was always told if you can't handle the turbulence of an airplane at 10,000 feet then you will not survive with the turbulence of an airplane at 30,000 feet. The most important thing is, do not allow your pain and your hurt to detour you.

One of the things the Lord gave me years ago that has been very helpful and instrumental in helping me cope and deal with some of the most horrific, painful seasons of my life is beginning to understand the pain of your present is going to prepare you for the blessings of your future.

As I study many of the patriarchs, prophets, kings, and writers of the Bible, I'm encouraged by how they dealt with their disappointment, pain and hurt. One of the greatest characters in the Bible we read about, who probably experienced more hurt than anyone else I know in the scriptures, of course, would be Job. I don't want to get into deep theology or commentary about his life, but there is a very important principle I do want us to consider. Those of you who have read the Book of Job probably know there are forty-two chapters. The highlight of Job's life is the conversation about him between God and Satan. Satan says to God, *"Job loves you and he serves you because there is a hedge about him, but if you remove the hedge and let me attack him Job will curse you to your face."* God permitted Satan to attack Job, not to prove Job's loyalty, because the Bible says he loved God and was a righteous man. Not to prove Job would be able to survive his pain and his challenges by losing everything, or to prove God was more important. I do not subscribe to those narratives. Actually, when you read the entire book of Job, it never answers the question why God permitted him to suffer. I remember when I went on a theological hunt trying to discover what was in the mind of God when he permitted Satan to attack the life of Job. I thought I would come up with a resolution or some answer to satisfy my curiosity why God would allow a man to go through so much pain and hurt. After much searching, the Holy Spirit finally spoke to me and said, *"It's not about why God permitted Job to suffer, the real question is can you trust God when the question why is never answered."* Wow. How many times do we go through hurt, we go through pain and disappointment and ask God the question, *why? Why did you take my loved one? Why didn't you help me in my storm? Why did you allow my children to suffer? Why did you allow my mother to pass with cancer?* Oftentimes, if we do not get the answers to our questions, it becomes difficult to move on and trust the sovereignty of God for future events that may occur in life. Sometimes, out of love and respect for God, we move quietly but, in our hearts, we are resenting God. I've had to deal with the question, *why so much hurt in my childhood? Why so much hurt in my family? Why the pain and the disappointment of not knowing who my biological father was and, even when I found out, how can you be a preacher and disown me as your son?* Yet, God never answered the question why. He just commanded me to forgive without any explanation, and without answering any of my questions. He says just forgive. So, the challenge for all of us is simply this, when you are hurting, when you're going through disappointment and pain, can you still trust God when the question, why, is never answered. It is the sovereignty of God because nothing ever catches God by surprise.

The 3 D's of Destiny

It is amazing how sunshine, and rain are required to make a beautiful flower grow. Now as a man looking back through my life, seeing different segments when I didn't think I would survive because of the depth of the hurt and the pain, God knew all the time that one day it would be a powerful testimony. I would be able to shout and praise and give glory to God because I survived something I didn't think I could. One of the things I've learned is this, do not let your hurt and your pain distract you from staying on the path to your purpose and your destiny. A principle the Lord taught me is what I call the 3 D's of destiny. The first one is "Detours," the second one is "Distractions," and the third is "Delays." A *detour* is an alternate route other than the route God has chosen for your life. Sometimes when we go through pain and hurt, we want to take a different route. We don't want to go through the pain. We want to find a route that relieves us of that, but, oftentimes, manifestation of what God is going to do in your life is through and not around. You have to say to yourself, *"I will not take a detour, but I will suffer through it."* The second D is *distractions.* Distractions are people, places and things we put in front of God. Distractions can cost us valuable time because we're too busy and preoccupied trying to please people. Trying to make people happy, or trying to make people understand us, who we are and why we do what we do. Time is the currency of life. It is a commodity that once it is lost, can never be regained. Another great lesson I've learned is when God has spoken a preordained, predestined word over your life, Satan cannot stop it. But, he can distract you if you let him. The third D is *delays.* Delays are when God is preparing us spiritually, physically, mentally, emotionally by allowing us to go through learning curves, challenges and experiences in life. To mature and prepare us so, when we get to the mountain top of our blessing, in the manifestation we'll have the tools we need to deal with the challenges at that level. Sometimes what God will do is hold up the blessing until our character matures and grows to a level where we can handle it. God will not take you where your character cannot keep you. It is easier to fall three feet than it is to fall twenty feet. Sometimes God is waiting for us to develop. And, the sooner we do, the sooner He can release blessings to help us get to our purpose and destiny.

I've also learned when God is preparing you, it doesn't take Him years to prepare your blessing. Whatever God has spoken over your life is already done. It's completed. God doesn't take years of development to prepare it *for* you, but to prepare *you* for it. We desire to walk in the manifestation and fulfillment of our blessings, purpose and destiny right now, which can be very painful. We need to look at the other side of it and learn how to praise God and rejoice that He did not release too much too soon. What should have been a blessing to us, because we were ready and prepared, has become our spiritual demise.

I was thinking about David. The Bible says he was a man after God's own heart. It certainly couldn't have been because he was a perfect man. We know his flaws. David was never perfect in obedience, but he was perfect in repentance. In Psalm 51, I call it the Psalm of Repentance, David acknowledged his transgressions and God forgave him. On another occasion, David and his men were out in the field and when they came back to Ziklag, the city had been burned to ashes. As you may recall, I shared this story in great detail at the end of Chapter 7, how in biblical times the grieving process involved putting on sackcloth and ashes. Sackcloth and ashes symbolically represented their grief, pain and hurt. Like David, many times we've had to go through hurt and the grieving process, which is really a part of life. Ecclesiastes teaches us there is a time to mourn and a time to laugh. What inspired me the most about David is in the midst of his pain, his heart and his grieving. The Bible says he grieved, he sat in sackcloth and ashes seven days. After the seventh day, he inquired of the Lord asking, *"Should I pursue after the Amalekites?"* The Lord responded to him saying, *"Pursue and in your pursuit, you will recover all."* What speaks to me about this is, it is okay to grieve, it is okay to feel your pain, it is okay to feel your hurt because you are human. But at some point, you've got to take off the sackcloth, brush off the ashes and pursue! David grieved seven days and I want to prophetically speak to someone right now. "You've been grieving, you've been hurting too long. It's time to brush off the ashes because you will never reach your dream. You will never experience purpose and destiny sitting in your ashes depressed and filled with anxiety because of what you've had to deal with in life and how people have wounded and hurt you." David pursued and in his pursuit the Lord said, *"You will recover all."* A very important lesson I've learned about God is He does not bless people standing still. He blesses people in motion, and so, my friend, brush off your ashes. Brush off the ashes of your dream and your vision, your purpose and destiny. I know you have failed several times but so did Michael Jordan, so did the Wright brothers, but they brushed off the ashes. Now the world knows who they are because they refused to grieve and hurt for a lifetime. Do not let your pain define who you are, you are bigger than your pain, it is a part of the process. Brush off the ashes.

In writing this chapter, I think about my past. I've had to brush off the ashes in many different circumstances and situations. One that comes to mind happened when I was about fifteen years old. I became a member of Greater Faith Temple Church of God in Christ. That's the church my mother joined where Bishop E.T. Foreman was the pastor. My mother told him, *"My son has been preaching since he was eight years old and I've done all I can do. Now I want you to take him under your wing and help him to continue to grow."* I will never forget that! He told her he would take on that responsibility. Being a musician, I became the church organist and played every Sunday. Bishop Foreman was, what we used to call, a long-winded preacher—meaning it was nothing for him to preach for two hours. There were times I would even travel with him as his musician. We would go to Virginia and New Jersey, sometimes New York. I never felt him to be a father figure. I don't know why. I guess it's because there were times, I felt there was such a difference between who I was and who many of the other young men in the church who the Elders. I felt like I never really measured up to his standard. Even when he allowed me to preach, I never felt validated or encouraged. Of course, Bishop was an old school preacher. All he needed was one verse of scripture and he would preach a whole sermon on that scripture.

Once he said to me, *"I want you to do the service on Sunday nights."* The service was an outreach and, because I was good with organizing and bringing people together, it really grew. Prior to that, we only had a small group of people who would come back to Sunday night service.

Bishop Foreman was really excited! That's what I saw, joy on his face as the service grew. One Sunday night he said, *"I'd like to have remarks."* So, he made his remarks, and we went back into service. I would invite a lot of groups to come. It was really a young people's service because I was young. Then there was this one service. There were a lot of people in attendance leaving the sanctuary close to full. I guess that night Bishop Foreman really got excited and said, *"I'm gonna have words again."* This time it went from words to preaching. I mean he preached and, of course you know, I started to feel some kind of way because he had given me the service to create for young people. Now, after I built it up, without saying anything, he took it back. Well, he is the pastor and can do whatever he wants, but I just thought it would have been fair for him to say something, or explain it to me. That was the beginning of me feeling like my gift and anointing, I'm not sure if I want to say, he was intimidated by it.That's the way I felt. There were times I would preach, and people were really blessed. Then he would get up and downplay my sermon, like it really wasn't all that good. I got to a point where I really didn't even want to preach. I couldn't explain it all, but I do know one thing, there was no reason for me to leave the church feeling hurt after I gave my all. Instead of being encouraged by my spiritual father, I was discouraged.

One day I went on a trip with another pastor in Florida. I was his musician for a weeklong revival. We stayed at one of the mother's homes midweek. I was standing in the backyard where there was a little pond in the middle of this whole neighborhood. In the middle of the pond was dirt you would have to swim to. All of a sudden God gave me a vision. At the time, I must have been about eighteen or nineteen years old. This dirt in the middle of the pond appeared to be an island. I saw sick people, hungry people. I saw people who were hurting and sinners who weren't saved and needed Christ and the gospel. The Lord spoke to me in this vision and said, *"I'm going to use you to be a blessing and to build a bridge to these people."* Man, I'd never experienced that in my life. Later that night at church, as we were in worship, I got the idea that God wanted me to pastor a church. When I got back home to Delaware, I told my pastor I believed God was calling me to pastor a church. The look he gave me I can still see when I close my eyes today. As I look back on this circumstance as an older man, and having preached for fifty-four years, I think the appropriate thing he should have done was said something like, *"Son just because God showed you a vision about helping people and that he was going to use you as a pastor, doesn't mean right now. Sometimes God gives us visions and dreams about what we're going to become so let me help you. Let me train you, let me teach you."* That's what should have happened. Then I wouldn't have done what I thought in my elementary mind at the time. I think that's the difference between not being intimidated by someone's gift, talent, or anointing. I felt like he went into defense mode. He had to do something because now I, this young man, was getting ready to go back to church and he didn't want his young people or his members to go. I never thought like that, but now as I look back on it and see, I did. I went and found the building and fixed it up. What I did know is he had a meeting with the church and the youth and dared them to not go or come to my church. I didn't know that for three years! I pastored the church for five before God moved me to California to go to college.

My point is, I was hurt by one of my spiritual fathers who could have sat me down and said, *"Let me help you."* When I tried to invite him to come preach, he would never come. I never knew the young people were told not to visit the church until years later, after the church was over and I was in California. A young person actually told me, who was at that meeting. My point is, I could have been so wounded and so hurt. I could have left church and done something altogether different, but there was a love for God in me deeper than any pain I could ever experience. So, I brushed off the ashes and kept moving forward. I remember when he got sick several years later. He was experiencing Alzheimer's, and I used to go to his house to sit with him. For moments at a time, he would remember who I was, and we would talk. I would sit there looking at him and thinking to myself, *"I thank God I didn't become bitter. I thank God I didn't allow the pain and the disappointment of one of my spiritual leaders to incarcerate me and cause me to forfeit my dream, my purpose and my destiny."*

I do admit now God was calling me to training, not to a church. Five years after I birthed the church, I had to shut it down because the building was condemned, and we had nowhere to go. Plus, God was leading me to California to go to Bible college. God said, *"I want to train you, I want to teach you."* I followed God's directive and finally graduated with my doctorate in church administration and my master's in biblical counseling. When we birthed Frontline Ministries in 2003, that was God's timing!

Sometimes our pain and hurt can be self-inflicted because we heard God, we just didn't flow with the timing of God. At the end of the day, the Bible is right, *all things do work together for the good to them that love the Lord and to those who are the called according to his purpose.* God will take every experience you will ever go through in life and use them to prepare you for where He's taking you. You just have to be ready to walk with Him through the fight, through the fire, through the flood, through the rain, and be confident that, *"He which hath begun a good work in you will perform it until the day of the Lord Jesus Christ."*

Great Pain Comes Through People

For anyone in pursuit of purpose and destiny, the fulfillment of your God-given dreams will constantly have to be adjusted. Unfortunately, this also includes people. Some of the greatest pain you will ever feel will come through people, particularly from those whom you love. Everybody is not ordained to go where God is taking you. Sometimes, when you try to make people a part of what God has called you to, it will hinder you from getting there. You have to make those adjustments. So many people have come and gone from my life, I used to question, *"Is it me?" "Am I not a good friend?" "How have I contributed to losing this person in my life?"*

Life will teach you that people are like scaffold and rocket boosters. Why? Because sometimes God places people in your life for a season. When you think about a rocket, you have the launching pad and then you have the rocket boosters. The launching pad becomes like the leaning post for the rocket. As they're building it, you know it's connected to the launching pad. Then the rocket boosters are going to help give the rocket its thrust into orbit. The thing about the launching pad and rocket boosters is they were not created nor designed to go the distance. When the countdown ends and that rocket leaves the launching pad, the launching pad cannot go. As a matter of fact, the season for the launching pad is over. Sometimes people are like launching pads. They are there to help stabilize you; to help build you but are not designed to go where God is taking you. Then there are the rocket boosters. All that fire and smoke being produced is really not from the rocket, it's from the rocket boosters. When the rocket boosters get to a certain distance and use up all its thrust, they are designed to fall off. Now the rocket can continue into orbit to reach its target. It took the launching pad and the rocket boosters to help launch the rocket, but they both were not designed to go the distance. Herein lies the principal. When the rocket boosters use up all its force, power and thrust, they do not fall off, what was designed to be an asset now becomes a liability. It becomes a weight to the rocket. One scripture written by the Apostle Paul says, *"Lay aside every weight and sin that doth so easily beset us."* We know what sin is, but the weight doesn't necessarily mean sin, it just means anything that can hinder you from maximizing your potential and going where God is taking you. That's where the rubber meets the road, the difficult task. Sometimes you have to admit to people God used them for a season, and they were the launching pad or they were the rocket booster. Sometimes people just assume investing in your life gives them lifetime rights and privileges to be with you and to go wherever you go. That's not true. You've heard the saying, *"It's lonely at the top."* Not everyone is designed to be there. Many are called but few are chosen. Now the only thing you owe to the "launching pad" and "rocket booster" people in your life is gratitude. Thank you, two words. Just, *"Thank You."* You owe them nothing more than that. Of course, people will always say you wouldn't be who you are and where you are if it had not been for them and what they did. I don't think you should take the time to argue the fact. Just respond with two words, *thank you.* Sometimes people will try to make you feel indebted to them, so they always come with a handout, as if you created a debt with them that you could never repay. That's the exact reason why everybody can't go where God is taking you.

I think one of the worst things you could experience is to have someone you call your best friend, yet unbeknownst to you they are jealous of you. I had a friend like that who finally one day said to me, *"You know my dad told me not to hang around you and that you would never amount to anything. I admire you now because I live one mile up the street from my dad and you're in California pursuing your dream."* That hit me in the pit of my gut because I would never have believed his father would ever say that about me. I never thought he was that kind of person, and I never believed my friend, my best friend, would not tell me about that in years prior. But then he said something to me, *"I have always been jealous of you."* How do you respond to that? When it is someone you would give your blood to, someone you would give the shirt off your back to. I wasn't angry. I was hurt and devastated because I never had a father. To have close friends like that, when I achieve a milestone for something great that would happen in my life. Like a son who wants to tell his dad. I didn't have a father, so the closest thing was my friend. It got to a point where I could tell from the response, he didn't sound so happy about my success. We got to a point where I would talk to him and he would ask me how things were going, and I would downplay things. It could have been something really spectacular that just happened and I was dying to tell him, but because I knew the kind of response I would get, I wouldn't share it.

Anyone who's ever had a best friend, you know no one can hurt you like a best friend can. I remember one day I was so lonely in California because I had no friends. Only constituents, people I worked with, yes, but not a friend I grew up with from childhood. One day I missed my friend so I called him. His wife answered the phone, and I asked to speak to him. She knew who I was, and I heard her tell him, *"Norman's on the phone."* He didn't know, and he still does not know to this day, that I heard his response through the phone. He said, *"I do not want to talk to him."* That was a hurt and pain I can't describe. Looking back, I now understand everybody can't go where God is taking you. Sometimes when you have a friend who desires to do the same thing you're doing, and you're excelling at it, but they're not. It takes a real friend. I've never been the kind of friend not to help. Sometimes you may have friends who don't want your help because they don't want it to be said that you helped them. I've been hurt by every best friend I ever had, If I stood before a judge to testify, everything I've ever done was to help them. I can't apologize for being gifted. I can't apologize for being anointed. I can't apologize for the zeal and the desire inside of me to pursue. I didn't have a silver spoon or favor from man on earth. I only walked in the grace and the favor of God.

I'm saying all of this to somebody who's listening or reading this book; you do not have to make excuses to anyone who has become jealous and envious of you. You weren't willing not to pursue so, yes, it is lonely at the top. People see your glory, but they do not know your story. Over time I have learned to be content, to be happy, not because of things, but because of God. Because I am fulfilling my purpose and destiny, lives are being blessed, and people are being changed. They are encouraged and inspired through my work and ministry. So, if loneliness is a part of the price I must pay, then so be it. All I know is, more than ever now, I just want to please God.

Have you heard this saying, *hurt people hurt people?* I do believe that, but I also believe *healed people, heal people.* When you learn to forgive people for the hurt they have caused you, then, and only then, will you experience victory over your pain. Some people spend a lifetime trying to make other people feel the way they make them feel. They try to make people feel the way they felt. I guess I said it right, I don't know. But once you've been healed from hurt and you're able to articulate, document, understand and explain it. Then you are able to use it as fuel on the testimony to help someone else.

If anybody knows how to overcome painful circumstances and situations Lord knows I've got some trophies of pain. I never let it define me and I never let what people felt or thought about me determine how I'd respond to them. I guess I'm different. If half the people who owe me money would pay me back, I could probably buy a $2,000,000 house with cash. Yet, I've forgiven all of them and still speak to them. I just do business a different way now.

I was young when I pastored my first church, New Hope Church of God in Christ in Laurel, Delaware. At the time, my Superintendent's church was maybe four miles from my church. He had been pastoring for probably twenty years with about ten members. When I birthed my church, even though it was located in a small town, we were growing rapidly. In the first month or so we were up to almost fifty members. Word got around and, when he heard about it, he complained to the state Bishop. I believe because they were friends, I received a letter from the state Bishop saying I had to move my church because it was too close to his. They even decided there was some law in our denomination handbook, which really was not there, but I didn't know at the time. So, I started looking around trying to figure out where to go. We were living in an apartment at the time and certainly didn't have room for our congregation. No one else in the church had a house big enough. I went around to some of the other pastors to see if I could use part of their church or a different service time. They all said no.

Then I received word that my Superintendent was in the hospital. Apparently, he had a mild heart attack. Even though I knew he had gone to the state Bishop and complained about me, out of honor and respect I went to the hospital. When I walked in the room he was laying there in the bed conscious. He saw me, I spoke to him and we started conversation. After I told him I was praying for him, he started asking me questions about the church. He said, *"How's your church going?"* and I said, *"Well the church is doing pretty good but we've gotta move."* Out of the clear blue he said to me, *"Why don't you bring your people over to my church and you can pastor that church."* I couldn't believe what I was hearing. Apparently, he was planning on retiring after the heart attack, but I responded to him saying, *"Superintendent, I didn't come here to talk to you about this, I just came to check up on you to see how you're doing."* I changed the conversation, prayed with him and left. They were having service every Sunday night, and we weren't. So, the following Sunday evening I decided to stop by. He was still in the hospital. His wife was there and maybe about ten people, no more than ten including me. Back then, we used to have testimony service where everybody would sing a song and then testify. His wife stood up and started testifying. He must have had a conversation with her about me bringing our people to his church. She started testifying and said, *"This so-called pastor, Elder Hutchins, had the nerve to go to the hospital while my husband was on his sick bed and asked him for his church."* I'm sitting there looking at her like, *"What? No, that's not quite how that went."* When I tell you this woman lit into me in front of these people. I mean she fussed at me, and I just sat there and didn't say one word. When I walked out after the service, man, I felt abandoned, I felt pain, I felt...oh my God, I felt so many emotions. I didn't know what to do. It wasn't about maybe a week or so later we got a note on our church door, which was a storefront underneath apartments. Apparently, the city had condemned the apartments upstairs because they needed a lot of repairs, and they gave us sixty days to vacate. I couldn't find anywhere to go, and our search time was low. I said, *"God, what am I going to do?"* Mind you, now, this was prematurely in terms of me being a pastor because I thought when God gave me that vision about me helping people and pastoring that it meant then. It was really just God letting me know that's what my purpose and destiny would become. In His permissive will, He allowed me to do that, but God has a way of closing doors and then opening doors. It reminds me of one of the banks I did business with in Delaware. They had this safety feature, a security system. The way it worked, to get inside the bank you had to go through two doors. Once you went through the first door there was a small core door, and the second door would not open until the door behind you closed. You can pull on it and pull on it but it will not open until the door behind you closes. Then you could open the door in front of you. Sometimes God is just like that. He will not open a door in front of you until the door behind you is completely closed. That's what I was in the process of experiencing, but I didn't know it at the time.

Finally, I'm trying to find a place to take our congregation when, all of a sudden, I got a phone call from a brother I knew and hadn't heard from or seen in several years. He was in the Navy and stationed in Fontana, CA. He said to me, *"You should come to California! This is where you need to be!"* He knew I loved music and that I was a pastor. I always wanted to go to Bible college, and, back then, I was in love with Fred Price Ministries located in Los Angeles, CA. I thought this would be a great opportunity for me to go to Crenshaw Christian Center, pursue my music, and he would help me. He would give me and my family a place to stay and help us get our own place. I prayed about it and in two weeks I remember having the last conversation with the church. I told them we were going to shut the church down because the building had been condemned and we have nowhere to go, but God was leading me to California. I told them I was going to Bible college, but coming back one day. It felt like a funeral. The church was dominated by my family. Many of my sisters, nieces and nephews really made up the church, and they cried and cried.

So, I moved away to California and that was the beginning of a long, winding road that would eventually lead me back home twenty years later to birth Frontline Ministries. What is amazing is everyone who cried when I left, none of them are members at the church today. There's a lesson to learn here. Never let anyone hold you hostage where you are to please and satisfy them. By faith you must trust God and step out. Go where He sends you. This reminds me of the Israelites. Their job was to follow the cloud. The Bible calls it the Shekinah glory cloud. He was a pillar of fire by night and a pillar of cloud by day. The importance of following the cloud is, there were always three things in it: the presence of God, the anointing of God and the provisions of God. Life has taught me as long as those three things are present, you know you're under the right cloud. If you're not experiencing those things, then you need to get under the right cloud. Don't be led or guided by people. Be led by the Shekinah glory cloud God has for your life. In it you will always experience the presence of God, the anointing of God, and the provisions of God.

CHAPTER TEN

JOURNEY OF FORGIVENESS

In the book of Matthew chapter 18, Peter asked Jesus a question and also attempted to answer it at the same time. He said to Jesus, *"How often shall someone sin against me and I forgive him, seven times?"* and Jesus responded to him and said, *"Not seven times but seventy times seven."* Now, of course, if you do the math that would be four hundred and ninety times in one day. In essence, what Jesus was saying as often as your brother or anyone, as far as that is concerned, sins against you, you are to forgive them. Forgiveness for the believer is also a biblical law. The Bible says if you do not forgive men their trespasses neither will your Father in heaven forgive your trespasses. The danger of harboring unforgiveness in your heart and not obeying the command to forgive, is that unforgiveness can breed resentment, bitterness and hatred. The human body is not designed to house these characteristics. So, the body responds to bitterness, anger and resentment in physical form. That's why many people become sickly, because they refuse to forgive.

Forgiveness is not always easy, particularly, because of the pain and disappointment that is associated with it. Not forgiving is like having a wound that will never heal. Once you forgive and release the pain, over time, especially when God is involved, and you give it to Him, you will heal. It's like a cut on your arm. A fresh cut is painful but, eventually, when it heals you still have the scar. You just don't feel the pain. One of the ways you can tell if you have honestly and truly forgiven someone who has offended or wounded you in any way is you can be in their presence or even talk about it and not feel the pain associated with it. If you see them and feel emotions, or if can talk about it and get angry, sad or even want to cry, then this is not a sign total forgiveness. True forgiveness has not taken place. Life is a journey of forgiveness. You have to know how to manage it so it doesn't distract you from experiencing the joys and fullness of life.

People who offend you oftentimes move on with life and leave you stuck at the place of the offense. Not only have they offended you, but your lack of forgiving them has become like the bars of a castle, keeping you locked out of God's best blessings for your life. My life has been a journey of forgiveness, not because that's my personality or the kind of person I am, but because I love God and honor His Word. I've been offended, and I've been wounded. There are several things in my life I had to process and forgive. A lot of people think forgiveness means continuing fellowship with the person or persons who've wounded you, and pretending things are normal, but that's not true. If a snake bites you once it is the snake's fault. But, if it bites you twice, it's your fault. Forgiveness doesn't mean you have to maintain close friends or even a relationship with your offender or those who have wounded you. It simply means you forgive them, but you move on. You are cordial to them when you see them. You do not talk about them in a negative way to other people. True forgiveness doesn't always mean total restoration as family or friends. It means I'm not going to take the weight and baggage of unforgiveness into the next chapter of my life. Sometimes forgiveness is difficult because of the intensity of the pain and how deep it felt in the moment. After you process it, it will be to your benefit. It would be wise to forgive.

Sometimes we are blindsided by life and even people. You ask the question, *"Where did that come from? What did I do to deserve this response?"* One journey of forgiveness for me was so painful. I had a spiritual son who to this day I love very dearly. I treated him like he was my biological son. As a young preacher growing up in the church, he looked to me as his spiritual father, and I enjoyed his presence. As an anointed young man, I was trying to encourage him to grow in knowledge and in wisdom. In many ways, he reminded me of myself when I was his age. As years passed and God was changing my season as a pastor, the Lord showed me he would become my successor. God confirmed it, not just through me but through him, and we began the process of making the transition. I presented him to the church and, in the beginning, no one wanted to embrace him. With my endorsement and my continuing week after week, encouraging the people and being there to support him as he preached, the people warmed up to him. In the process, the Lord was leading my wife and I to move back to Los Angeles to birth Frontline West Coast. He was my successor preaching every Sunday and I had this big vision, this big dream that was filling my heart with so much joy. I told him I could see us traveling back and forth between Frontline East Coast and Frontline West Coast. We jokingly said that one day we would pass each other in the airport.

That was a vision I wanted to see come to fruition but, in the process, I was having some development challenges. This was not his first time pastoring a church. He pastored before I even did the dedication, but for many reasons the church did not survive. Still, he had great potential, and eventually Frontline East Coast began to embrace him. I would come home and share during the week because I was birthing the Frontline West Coast church in Inglewood, CA and was unavailable to be there on Sundays. He and I talked regularly. Often some of the toughest things I had to deal with were watching the service on Facebook or YouTube. I felt like it was developing a new sound too soon. The wisdom of a young man who is becoming a successor to anyone who has established ministry for any length of time, wisdom should teach them to change nothing. Flow with the heart of the ministry and do not try to change anything. Maintain, and at some point in time, once you become the pastor and God gives you innovative ideas, that would be the time. But don't change in the middle of transition. It's not wise for any preacher, whether you're young or old.

It got to the point I would come and visit, and I started feeling like a stranger at my own church. He treated me like I was a visiting pastor. One day I told him, *"You do not call me pastor in front of the people. They need to understand there is unity between you and I."* At the end of the day, I think it was his zeal, desire and, of course, youthfulness that caused him to implement different things. Because of my love for the people and the longevity my wife and I had birthed in the ministry, it was critical to know that if I were to leave it in his care, certain things would be in place. I had concerns. Not once did any of my apprehensions concern me so much I'd change my mind about him pastoring the church. I just needed him to get it and learn to make the adjustments. I shared with him that he had to be able to minister to a broad audience. I wanted his level of maturity to attract people from every class and ethnicity. There were things he did understand, but there were major things he did not. We went head-to-head on these issues. He was very adamant about what he thought was right and I felt was wrong. If you are going to be the successor to a seasoned pastor who is willing to turn everything over to you, the complete ministry, all of the history, all of the years, and everything he built, there should be a level of humility. You should not seek to change the structure midstream. I know you have a vision but no one who is a successor and preaches in the absence of the pastor should implement anything without his knowledge and approval.

This became a major problem. It got so that in certain areas I did not recognize the church my wife and I had established. Out of concern I had a private meeting at my house with the executive board. I told them the meeting was private, and I didn't want him to know about it. At the time he was in Atlanta, GA, and that was another big problem for me. When I made him my successor he was living in Philadelphia. The commute to the church was only an hour and twenty minutes. Now he is in Atlanta, and that's a flight. My concern was, there would be Sundays he would not make it. I told him I just didn't believe it was wise for him to be a long-distance pastor. He disagreed. My concerns to the executive board was trying to get him to understand. I felt he wasn't embracing certain details of importance. I was really looking for their opinions and advice. I started the meeting out by saying, *"If today was the day I was to appoint him as pastor, it probably wouldn't happen."* It did not mean I wasn't going to ever make him pastor, but the process, the training, was going to be much longer than I had anticipated.

Unbeknownst to me, someone in that meeting went and told him we had a private meeting, and I was thinking about not making him pastor. The person who told him was later identified. His response was he didn't tell me he knew about the meeting. He had been preaching now for over a year and could feel and sense the people's support and loving for him. Rightfully so, because he has a wonderful personality and reminded me of myself. There were people who used to tell me, *"Bishop, I can't stay because his level of preaching doesn't reach me the way yours did all the years I've been here."* That was understandable, but later on those same people said, *"He grows on you,"* and they became faithful to his preaching and leadership. One of the biggest challenges was things were changing, and the congregation assumed he had permission from me to make these changes. So, whatever he implemented and whatever he did, they agreed to and fell in line with it. Not knowing that after that meeting, he and I had very little conversation. I would confront him about making choices and decisions without my approval. I tried to figure out what had happened. Why has he changed toward me? One thought was, okay, so I'm in Los Angeles preaching every Sunday and can't come back to Delaware. So, he's taken ownership and done things without my permission. I reminded him I was still the pastor and saw, by his response, he felt he had the people's favor. When I confronted him about his style of preaching and the people he placed up front, who did not represent the posture or the style of the ministry, he took offense. On a strange phone call one day he asked me, *"When are you going to make me pastor?"* I wondered what motivated the question.

We were in the process of remodeling our new sanctuary and ran into some glitches with the city. Also, our realtor and the owner of the building died. So, we put a hold on the project until I could guarantee all the investment and work we put into the new sanctuary would be honored by the new people who would be in charge. At that point, we had invested over $280,000 into our new sanctuary, and I didn't want a new owner not to honor our contracts. We were leasing to buy. Once we got into the new sanctuary, the vision was to raise the funds and pay off the building. What I did not know is my spiritual son was building a private staff of people behind the scene. I'm preaching in Los Angeles still trying to figure out how he turned left. I didn't know he knew about the meeting and, apparently, he assumed I wasn't going to make him pastor. I had too much invested. When he asked me on that strange phone call when was I going to make him pastor, I answered him saying, *"Just be patient. You know what the vision is. I want us to complete the sanctuary so we can have a big celebration. We can do two things at one time. We can have our dedication in the sanctuary, and I can appoint you as pastor at the same time."* He dropped a seed and said, *"If you do not make me pastor, I just want you to know that I feel called to pastor here in Delaware Dover, particularly where the church is."* When he said that my heart dropped to my feet. I didn't know what to think or how to respond, but I knew that the man with me was giving me an ultimatum. That wasn't wise for a young man who was to be the successor of a wonderful ministry. As a matter of fact I remember when we celebrated our first year of grossing $1,000,000. His spiritual father was going to give him a ministry that had the potential to be financially lucrative for the community, for the church and for him. Yet now he was giving me an ultimatum because he did not want to wait! To try and help things along I said, *"I tell you what. This is what I will do. I can come to Delaware and make you campus pastor. I'll still be pastor, you can be campus pastor, and then later on in the year, once we complete the sanctuary I'll come and appoint you as pastor."* His response was a clear, *"I decline."* I didn't know what to do. I had no other options and no other preacher at the church to take his place, and he knew that. I felt like he was strong arming me. My response to him was, *"Listen, let's not deal with this right now. Let's just pray and God will work everything out."*

I shared with my wife what happened, and we started praying. My prayer was that I would get another phone call, and he would say, *"I'm sorry can we continue the plan."* I never got that call, so I phoned him, and he finally responded. We had choice words with me ending the conversation with, *"Since you decline, I accept your resignation,"* not knowing what I was going to do. He just said okay and hung up. I was in my head asking myself, *"What was I doing? Was I reversing the strong-arm technique thinking he would call back and say can we work this out?"* Quite naturally I would have. It was always my desire to make him pastor of the church. I just wanted him to understand there is protocol, a proper way of doing things. If I was his spiritual father, he could not treat me like I was his son. On pins and needles, I told him he did not have to come back to the church, and I'd have someone preach that Sunday. That didn't mean forever. I just wanted him to take a break to think about it. Hopefully, he would call me, but he had things in place and people on staff who he had been talking to. He was prepared to birth his own church less than five miles from our location.

I had no clue and no idea what was happening the Sunday I had someone else preach. We had a wonderful service in Los Angeles. After church, we were on our way to have lunch, and I started getting phone calls. My phone was blowing up! People were calling me, deacons were calling me, board members were calling me because at the end of the service my spiritual son and his entourage, his family, and many of the people who were on his side walked into sanctuary and down the center aisle.

He walked up to the pulpit, took the mic and said he was told not to ever come back. He proceeded to say things that were not true. I was told it was pandemonium in the sanctuary! Remember now, he had been preaching to these people for over a year. It only takes three months, if you are a good preacher, to turn the hearts of the people toward you. Three thousand miles away from the church that we birthed, and he's telling people things that were not true. My son! This reminds me of the story of David and his son Absalom. Absalom was trying to take over his father's throne not realizing his father loved him dearly and would have given him the throne eventually. Absalom was hung from a tree by his hair and stabbed with daggers. When David found out, even though he knew his son was trying to deceive him and take over his throne, he grieved his death. He said, *"My son, my son, would to God that I had died for you, my son. How I love thee, my son."* I felt like David when my spiritual son did that. My wife and I got on a plane and flew that Sunday night, and on Tuesday I had a meeting with the entire church. The atmosphere was different. I wasn't treated like a pastor or even the founder who birthed the church. More than seventy-five percent of the people left the church. Not everyone went with him but quite a few did. The church suffered financially, and I could not keep the doors open. I gave the church to another young preacher who grew up with me, and that is a whole other story in itself. It became a double whammy, as what he did to me was worse than my spiritual son. He erased my name and my legacy.

Several months later maybe after about a year, I received a strange text from my spiritual son. The text said, *"Miss you, I need you."* I was totally surprised and shocked for a moment. I start responding because, what he didn't realize, I had forgiven him. I really did. Not only did I forgive him, but he can still make me laugh because he reminds me too much of myself. The truth is, we started communicating for a moment and were planning a visit. He was coming to Los Angeles, and we were going to spend time together. Ironically, we never talked about anything that happened. I did ask him one day, when were we going to address the elephant in the room, and he said, *"Well, when I get to Los Angeles we can talk about that."* The Holy Spirit spoke to me and said, *"You have forgiven him but you cannot open the door again."* That was painful because as deep as he hurt me and all that he said about me, and he said some bad things even online, I forgave him. I just wanted my son, and the Lord said to me, *"You cannot open that door again."* I even asked God why he brought David to my spirit, and He said, *"David committed trespasses and sin against God, but I still let him be king. But just because I let you be king doesn't mean that I have excused you of the sin, the trespasses."* So, the Lord said to me, *"I can bless your right hand and curse your left hand,"* and that's what he did to David. He said the sword would never leave David's house and there would always be bloodshed. If you study his life that's exactly what happened. All of his children, rape, incest and murder was the legacy of the House of David. He was blessed on the throne, but he was cursed in the house. I knew then what God was saying to me. God can bless you in your right hand and curse you in your left hand because the truth is it's not about you. It was about the people that suffered in the process. It was about the many people who left the church and never came back. There is a tremendous price to pay for that, but my testimony is I do not harbor any unforgiveness in my heart against my spiritual son. I still love him genuinely. Honestly, I was looking forward to seeing him and to fellowship with him. Even to this day, there's not a week that goes by that I do not think about it. I do not play when it comes to fellowship and relationships. When I'm in, I'm all in! Even though he was not my biological son, there was something about the way he called me dad. Not even my own biological sons had the same effect. My son, my son, absolutely my son, would to God that I had died for thee.

When you are true to the scriptures, the scriptures will be true to you. Forgiveness is not a feeling; it is an action that you perform and commit to.

Forgiveness is an Action

Even though you're hurting, and even though you feel pain, you choose to forgive. I was watching television one day, and I love to quote TV. This particular case, a young man had killed and raped a man's daughter. At the sentencing, the judge gave him life without parole. In the closing statements, the father had something to say to the young man, who not only took the life of his daughter but violated her sexually. In the process he said, *"I forgive you."* The young man who committed the heinous crime looked at him in disbelief as if to say, *"How can you forgive me for what I have done?"* I can identify with the father, not in the same way of someone taking a life of a child, but the principle is the same. When you've been hurt, when you've been wounded, when someone has violated you, it's the same pain and yet he forgave this young man. I like to think that one of the reasons he forgave this young man is because he refused to be imprisoned for life. So, when they handcuffed the young man and took him out of the courtroom, the father refused to be imprisoned with him. It would take some time for his heart to heal, but the process starts when you say I forgive you. My journey of forgiveness has taken me to some hard places that drew my pain and disappointment. I had to forgive. Love and forgiveness go together. You haven't really accomplished anything if you forgive a person, but can't say that you still love them. You do not have to love what they did or love their ways, but the Bible commands us to love. The Bible says blessed are you when, *"Men shall revile you and persecute you and shall say all manner of evil against you falsely for my namesake. Rejoice and be exceedingly glad for great is your reward in heaven."* So forgiveness is not just about forgiving your offender. It is also about making sure the pathway is clear. So when I leave this earth, your violation against me will not hinder me from spending eternity with God.

The greatest pain I've ever had to forgive is with someone back in the early 90s, after moving to Los Angeles, CA. I connected with a mega church with over twenty-five thousand people. The Lord blessed me, and I became the director of social services and the executive minister of music. It was such a blessing. I'd never seen anything like it. We were doing five services, and each service was packed to capacity. It was nothing for me to go into the sanctuary as I'm preparing to sing with the choir. My personal choir was one-hundred twenty voices, and we had five choirs. I chuckle sometimes when I think about passing by Denzel Washington and he says, *"Great job,"* or Stevie Wonder, *"When you gonna sing my song?"* Boy, was I in my world! I was doing what I felt I was called to do from a child and God had opened this door. Not only did I sing, but I preached. There were times I preached two and three services. It was a great experience.

Once we recorded a CD, and one of my songs became very popular. The record company that we were signed to offered me a recording contract. Now, you know I'm really excited because all the songs I'd been writing, I now had an opportunity to share them with the world. So now I'm balancing several responsibilities on the weekends. I am teaching music pretty much every Saturday, and we sing on Sunday. Through the week, Monday through Friday, I'm director of social services keeping office hours assisting the community financially. Now I am a new recording artist on a record label! Boy, I remember going to the company in Nashville, walking through the lobby and I look up on the wall. They had a wall for artists pictures. I saw Richard Smallwood, Daryl Coley, Sandra Crouch, Andraé Crouch, BeBe and CeCe, Carmen, Steve Curtis Chapman, and then my picture as the newest artist Norman Hutchins. It was amazing to see the vision and the dream come to fruition. When I put out my first CD, the promotion department was telling me I needed to be available to travel, to help promote my CD. I'm thinking how is this going to be possible because of my work schedule, but I had an idea. I was hired as a choir director over one of the largest choirs in the church. A year or so later I was hired as the assistant to the director of social services and later became the director. So, I thought maybe I should just resign from director of social services, that way I could be available through the week to travel, do promotions and get back by Friday. I could have my rehearsals on Saturday and then be available to do what we do all day on Sunday. I thought it was a great idea.

Looking back, I probably should have discussed it first with my leader, but what I decided to do was write a letter. In this letter I explained I needed time to promote this album and wanted to let them know I'd actually resigned as director of social services. I said nothing in this letter about minister of music, only director of social services. I gave the letter to my leaders assistant and didn't hear anything for about two weeks. One day I came to work and there was a letter on the desk. I opened it and the letter read, *"With much prayer I've considered your request. When I hired you as director of the choir and director of social services, I considered those two positions one and so by you resigning from one you're resigning from them both. Therefore, I receive your resignation."* Oh my goodness, my heart fell to my feet! At that time, I had a wife and three small kids, and this was my only income. I rushed down to my leader's office and was able to get right in and said, *"No, no, no, please, please this is not what I meant."* I did everything I could to reverse his decision, and he said, *"My decision is final."*

When I walked out of the door, I didn't know what to do. How do I take care of my family even though I have a recording contract with a record company? No one knows me, but what made matters worse, the congregation was told I was moving on to bigger and better things. I sat there and said nothing. They even had a banquet for me, I'll never forget it. It was like a celebration in a special area of the church. I'm sitting there looking at people laughing and rejoicing. The choir and everyone were eating food and having a good time, while I'm sitting there with my heart aching. No one really knew what happened behind closed doors and, because I loved and respected my leader so much, I would not put it out there. I do remember saying to him after I could not get him to change his mind, that I wouldn't do like other people who lose their job and leave the church, because this is where God led me.

After the celebration and banquet I would still come to church. I wasn't singing, I wasn't preaching, I was just sitting there. Weeks passed and people were kind of wondering what's really going. I even had people come to me and say, *"I thought you were going on to bigger and better things and, yet, it seems like you're here on Sunday."* So, what I started doing was stay home some Sundays to make it appear I was out of town. One day the Holy Spirit spoke to me and said, *"Get back in that church and do not leave until I tell you."* Now, mind you, being the executive minister of music and the director of social services has its privileges, especially parking. Can you imagine twenty-five thousand people in a day? We had special parking almost at the back door, but now I'm parking half a mile down the street. I can see it in my mind right now, no special entry. I was hurting every time I went to church, but knew I had to be there. Months passed, by this time, before I found a job at another church playing for one of their services. Monday morning they paid me $175 for that service, then I found another job recycling cans. I was the Recycler, which means people from the streets, lots of drug addicts and alcoholics would collect cans throughout the city and bring them to my weigh station. I would weigh their cans and give them a voucher. They could go to the store and cash it. I had a bin where I placed the cans and, during rainy days, I'd stand inside the bin, almost like being inside a big old trash can. From the choir stand, from my office to the trash can. One day I went to the pawn shop and bought me a small keyboard. I put it inside the bin, and when I had no customers I would play and write songs. I did what I could to take care of my family, but on Sundays I parked down the street, walked around the front and still sat in the pulpit area.

One day my leader was preaching, and I think the sermon was relative to what I had been going through. Towards the end of the sermon, he looked at me and said, *"Come do the prayer at the end of the sermon."* I was floored! I got up and did the closing prayer thinking maybe was a good time to set up a meeting to talk to him. The meeting was set for the following week. I went into his office apologizing, *"I'm so sorry, I'm so sorry, please forgive me. This is my life's ministry, this is all I know how to do and what I was born to do, please."* He sat there, looked at me and said nothing. I felt like I was begging for my job, but it didn't matter. That was a man, and I needed to take care of my family. I'm sure he thought about the fact that I was true to my word. I said, *"Just because you fired me, I'm not going to leave the church."* He said, "Let me pray about it." I left and was hopeful. Of course, by this time, I noticed someone else had my position. That's a whole different story in itself. Eventually, I got a phone call from the office requesting me to meet with my leader. He said because of his position as an overseer of many churches, he had a church in an area that needed a pastor. So until he makes his decision, I could go and preach on Sundays and the jurisdiction would give me financial compensation. Man was I excited because now I was able to work my jobs, preach on Sunday and still go to church. I did that for several months until one day I was summoned back to the office. My leader said to me, *"I want to make you pastor of that church."* For most young preachers that should have been a happy and exciting occasion—your spiritual father is ready to send you out to pastor a church. But, that's not how I felt. Even though I agreed, I felt like my father was getting rid of me. You've got to remember. I was already disowned by my biological father and, yet, God placed other men in my life. The one man who I looked to as my spiritual father but was my biological father at the same time. I felt like he was getting rid of me. I can see the day of the dedication. The mass choir came, and the church was packed to capacity. I'm marching down the aisle with my wife and our children, and I'm hurting inside. A great celebration was going on, yet I felt my father was getting rid of me. To make matters worse, the executive board or the trustee board at that particular church didn't like me at all. They did so many mean things to me and weren't doing anything to really help me financially. That was a part of my journey of forgiveness, because at the end of the day it never changed how I felt about my spiritual father. No matter how bad I felt, I wouldn't dishonor him. I respect him, even to this day, and forgave him. I could have done things differently for sure, but I thought it was the responsibility of a father to teach and train his sons. I felt so abandoned, but I didn't resent him. Even though I was pastoring another church, I was still going to special events and evening services. Things got so bad at that church, and the way I was treated. After five years I resigned. The craziest thing is God restored the relationship between me and my spiritual father. Because I hung around, he could tell I genuinely loved him and was willing to submit myself. I'm one of those sons he could call and, no matter what I'm doing, I would honor his request because he means just that much to me.

To this day, not only was our relationship restored, but he started calling me to come minister and preach. I remember preaching one Thanksgiving when Stevie Wonder sang before I preached, and it was amazing! I remember when he called me in the office and asked me to become Elder Green's assistant. Elder Green was the Assistant Pastor of the church. Around this time, the Lord was leading me to move back to my home state to pastor a church. I said to my leader, *"I'm honored you even felt I was capable of even doing this, but God is leading me back to Delaware."* I still can hear him laughing to this day. I've never loved a man genuinely and respectfully as I have this man. One day while I was preaching at church he asked, *"So, when are you going to invite me to come to Delaware?"* Jokingly, I replied, *"You do not invite a bulldozer when you're building a chicken coop."* He laughed as I continued, *"Because I know I'm probably only going to get one opportunity. I've got to maximize it, so I'll let you know."*

A few years passed, and I was at his church preaching. I asked him, *"Can I get you on the calendar because I'm ready for the congregation to meet my spiritual father. I talk about and emulate you so much, they just want to meet you."* He gave me a date but, surprisingly, it was almost a year later. It's amazing how fast that year went by. I set it up as a special day and called it "A Night With The Father." That is how we advertised it. By this time, he was the Presiding Bishop of the Church of God in Christ, so I wasn't just inviting my pastor. Now here comes the Presiding Bishop and I am not a Bishop, I'm just a son. Word got around and I told my parishioners, *"You may need to get here about 5:00 because if you get here at 7:00 you're not going to have anywhere to sit!"* We had a nice sized congregation, seating about eight hundred people at the evening of the service. I will never forget it. General Board Bishops, Pastors and Bishops from New York, New Jersey, Philadelphia, Baltimore, Washington DC,

Maryland, all around the Eastern Shore area came to hear the Presiding Bishop Charles E. Blake. I had the privilege of introducing him, my spiritual father. He stood, walked to the podium and in his salutation, he began to talk about my experiences at West Angeles. He said things about me I never knew was in his heart. I'm sitting there in amazement, but what really got me is when he told my congregation and everyone in the house, *"Norman Hutchins could have easily been my biological son."* Wow, that did it for me! Wow, wow, wow! Because I refused to let bitterness, resentment, and anger control me. Because I refused to let pride keep me from attending church. Yes, I was deeply involved up front all the time—singing and preaching. Yet one day it all stopped, and I refused to get out of place. Because of that, I can pick up the phone, call my father and hear his voice. I don't even have to say, *"Oh, Bishop, this is Norman."* When he picks up the phone he says, *"Hello Brother Hutchins."* That means my name is in his phone.

Back in 2023, I had a major event in Los Angeles CA called the Impact Awards. I was able to honor him as one of the founders of praise and worship, the style as we know it today. With the praise and worship leader and background singers singing song to song, involving the congregation, and Bishop was one of their founders! I love this man of God, and I thank God. My biological father forsook me, and God brought me all the way from North Carolina through Delaware, through Fontana to Los Angeles to meet one of the greatest men in the world! He is a spiritual giant, a Moses to a Joshua. I can honestly say I am the man I am today, the husband, the father, the preacher, the pastor, the Bishop, because God placed Bishop Charles Edward Blake in my life.

For the believer, forgiveness is not a choice, it is a command. Jesus says forgive and you shall be forgiven. So, whatever your journey of forgiveness is, wherever you are on the road of forgiveness, each time you refuse to forgive it hinders you from getting to your ultimate destination—your purpose. We all have been offended. We all have gone through seasons where we have been discouraged but forgiveness is one of the major keys to experiencing God's freedom. Think about this for a moment. Jesus came to the earth to die for the sins of the world. He came to establish the Kingdom of God and, yet, they did not believe who He was. When He announced that He was God in the flesh they said, *"Treason, blasphemy!"* and sought to kill him. Eventually, we see Him on the cross hanging between two thieves. One says to him, *"If you be the Son of God why don't you save yourself and us too?"* The other thief said to the other thief, *"We deserve to be here but this man has done no wrong."* He says to Jesus, *"When you come into your Kingdom would you remember me?"* At that moment in agony and pain, nails in His hands, nails in His feet, Jesus took the time to minister to the thief and He says to him, *"Today thou shalt be with me in paradise."* Before Jesus would die, He would forgive everyone who did what they did to Him. It is written in the scriptures. He says, *"Father forgive them for they know not what they do."* Now the way I look at it, if Jesus the Son of God can be crucified with nails in His hands and His feet, pierced in the side, a crown of thorns on His head, and can forgive those who crucified Him. Then I have no excuse, you have no excuse, we all have no excuse for not forgiving people who crucify us with their mouth, with their lips, with their words or even violating us in a physical way. Forgiveness does not only determine the level of the offense. Basically, what Jesus is teaching us is no matter how you have been offended, no matter how you have been wounded, the law of forgiveness says forgive. Sometimes you hear people say *I will forgive but I will not forget.* That would not be true forgiveness. What if Jesus said the same thing, *I forgive you, but I will not forget.* So, when you're in a challenge or in a storm, and you need God's help, He would say, *I forgive you, but I haven't forgotten.* What you did, all of our sins have been covered by the Blood of the Lamb. The Bible says, *"If we confess our sin God is faithful and just to forgive us and to cleanse us from all unrighteousness."* So, if Jesus, the son of God, can forgive, so can we.

CHAPTER ELEVEN

MEN, FATHER & MENTOR

I wonder how different my life would have been growing up if I had a man, a father, and a mentor. That would eventually come much later in adulthood, but as a child I did not have that example. I was so gifted and talented as a child. Men who gravitated to me most of the time were pastors with their own agendas. I first thought they gravitated toward me because they knew I was fatherless and needed an example and mentors. I looked up to many of them only to discover they had hidden agendas. They really just wanted to take advantage of my gifts, my talent and my anointing. Eventually, like Saul and David, when the women began to sing the song, *Saul has slain his thousands but David his tens of thousands.* Saul became jealous of David, which always seemed to have been the case with me. In my opinion, the way to get close to a pastor is to begin working in ministry. When people would sing my praises or have good things to say about who I am and what they perceived I would become, then the pastors' conversations would be something like, *"You gotta stay humble. Don't become prideful."* The truth is those thoughts were nowhere near my heart. I've always been a person of humility. Several times I could sense and feel their envy and jealousy. What I would do is retreat and eventually separate myself from them.

It's amazing how I thought I was an adorable child. One of the most embarrassing moments I remember is I'd been playing for a church for ten years. There was never any financial compensation, nor did I expect it. I was just happy to play and be a part of worship. One day the pastor said to the congregation, *"Elder Hutchins has been playing for us for over ten years now, and we want to be a blessing to him."* At the end of service, he told the ushers to take an offering plate and put it on the organ. Mind you now, I'm sitting there playing. Furthermore, he told the congregation, *"After the benediction, before you leave, I want you to march around and put something in the plate. Be a blessing to this young man."* He gave the benediction then asked me to play some music while people were marching. I started playing and people were coming around putting money in the offering plate that was on the corner of the organ. I heard the sound of nickels, dimes and quarters and maybe a dollar or two here and there. All of a sudden I had this image in my mind that I've seen several times on television of a man playing a music box while a little monkey was on the ground dancing. When people came by and put money in the box, the little monkey would tip his hat to the people. That's how I felt. It was so embarrassing. That happened almost forty years ago. When I talk about it to this day, I can still feel it. How disappointing it was to learn that was how my pastor felt about me. I've been disappointed by many men growing up in my life. There was one man, a White man, older gentleman named Reverend Val Miller. He was a preacher—short, bald, and a Mennonite. I made mention of him in Chapter Three. He was such a kindhearted man, and one people always took advantage of. I remember he was a contractor and a carpenter. Many of the Black preachers would use him to build houses and extensions on their churches and all kind of things and wouldn't pay him. Mind you, I'm a young man growing up, and this was my example of a man; not to be honest, not to take care of your financial responsibilities when you agree to do something. You have every right to renege. Time and time again, I would see him being taken advantage of. In my mind I thought, when I become a man, I do not ever want to be like that. I wanted to be honest and integral. I wanted to treat people right. People always say you become the example of what you see. I do not agree with that because I know what I saw and I know what I experienced, but I never felt it was right. To be honest, I think my biggest problem growing up was being just too gifted and talented. It seemed the men in my life, who were always preachers, were intimidated by my gift, talents and my anointing. As long as they could benefit from me, they treated me like I was a son. When it got to a point they could no longer benefit or profit from me, they abandoned me. I would go through rejection and feel the hurt, pain and disappointment for a while, then eventually here comes the next person. Thinking it would be better, it seemed like it got worse. I know we always say a woman cannot teach a boy how to be a man. The truth is my mother was probably more responsible for me learning how to be a man than any man I ever knew growing up.

One day in school, when I was about nine years old, this young girl I liked kissed me. After she kissed me, I was so afraid. I mean I cried, and I cried. The reason being I thought at nine years old, if you kissed a girl, she would get pregnant. So, when I got home my mother asked me, *"What's wrong, Norman?"* I mean I was sobbing and crying and didn't want to tell her, but she continued to ask and finally I said, *"Mom, I'm so sorry!"* She said, *"What are you sorry about?"* I said, *"I got a girl pregnant."* She gave me this look and said, *"What do you mean you got a girl pregnant?"* I told her, *"I kissed a girl at school and now she's pregnant."* I had never seen her laugh the way she did and was so puzzled and confused. Why would you laugh, and I just got a girl pregnant? That's when my mother explained to me that a kiss cannot get a girl pregnant. As they say, at some point, somebody has to teach you about the birds and bees. I always thought a man should discuss that with me, but because I had no man, no father, no mentor, it was my mother who told me. She taught me how to be a young man, and how to be respectful. I miss my mother.

Growing up in the 60s was really difficult especially when you would see White men disrespecting Black men. They would call them all kinds of names. I've heard them called "boy" and even the "N" word. I remember thinking, why doesn't the Black man talk back or say something to defend himself? It seemed like the Black man was the weak man, and the White man was the strong man. I remember thinking I didn't want to be weak. If they said something to me, I was going to say something back. I remember the first time a White man called me the "N" word. I must have been about eight years old. Two of my friends were with me in a store and I thought to myself, *I'm gonna call him a name.* He called me the "N" word, and I called him the "C" word for Cracker. Then they said all kinds of nasty things. We just ran home. I didn't like always seeing Black men being disrespected. My example of a man growing up, of course, was the man I thought was my father, who was really my stepfather. The alcoholic who was drunk ninety percent of the time and not a good example.

Having come from a very large family, being the baby boy of six boys on my mother's side and about seven brothers on my biological father's side, some of whom are deceased. Amazingly, not one brother of mine on my mother's side was an example of a man I could look up to or what a father should be. It seems like most of my brothers followed in the footsteps of their dad. They became alcoholics, didn't really work much and were always drunk. Today, I wonder why I didn't follow that path. How was it possible for me to grow up in such a negative environment, around male role models who were always negative and not turn out like them? I would meet powerful men who became my mentors in my mid-twenties, but why didn't I go astray? Why didn't I travel the path so many of the men I saw in my life travel? That question is sometimes difficult to answer. But in an attempt to answer it, I think it was television that helped find the answer—the power of TV. When we watched TV, especially seeing Black men for the first time in movies and commercials, it was wow! Even then it seemed like the role model of a Black man on television was struggling in life. One show everybody remembers, in particular, in the black community was *Good Times,* with J.J., Thelma, Michael, Mr. James Evans and his wife Florida. In the 60s and 70s, Mr. James Evans became the television role model of a man, but the problem I saw was he always seemed angry. He was never happy; he was always struggling financially trying to make ends meet and take care of the family. The power of TV had me feeling like he was who I would become. Growing older though, I began to realize it was just acting, and not reality. I didn't have to become my plight. I have free will, I have choices, and I can make decisions to succeed or fail.

One of the most powerful things about being a human being created by God is inside each and every one of us is the ability and capacity to be great! You can be influenced by what you see in positive or negative ways. If you see negative things, you can still be influenced by them, but you have to make a decision this is not the direction you are going. When you see positive things, you emulate that. As a child, I always loved to see professional looking men dressed up in suits, carrying their briefcases and doing business. I felt that's who I was supposed to be. As I got older, I would dress to impress and carry my briefcase when I went to school. So many times, I'd wear a suit, shirt and tie with my patent leather shoes and be asked where I was going. There was something about being dressed up that made me feel successful and like a businessman.

Man, This is What You Do

I had no man to sit me down and say, *"This is what you do, this is how you do it."* And, yet, somehow, some way, deep down inside I knew there was much more than what I saw. Now that I'm an adult, one of the things I look back and think about is, you do not have to become a victim of your environment.

We talk about culture, and how children oftentimes are molded and shaped by the culture they are in, which suggests you have to live a certain way, look a certain way and do certain things. I remember watching a movie called the *Bee Movie.* As small babies these bees were in school being trained. I mean thousands of bees, and they could talk! When they graduated from the Bee Academy the instructors took them on a tour of the beehive where they had to make a choice about what to do for the rest of their lives. The only problem was the beehive jobs were repetitive. If you decided you wanted to make honey, you did that job over and over, the same repetitious pattern every day. There was one particular bee who looked at every job and saw nothing that caught his attention. His friends said, *"Man, you got to pick something,"* but he looked outside of the beehive. He saw bees flying from the beehive out into the world, lighting on flowers, getting nectar and bringing it back to the hive. These bees got to experience life and see and do things. He said, *"That's what I want to be!"* They told him he couldn't, but he kept on and pursued until he was able to join that special force. That was me growing up. I've always thought outside of the box and never favored the norm. I saw what other people were doing and knew there had to be something different for me. That's the importance of having dreams and visions. They become your life's road map leading you to success. Men who God eventually placed in my life and taught me how to be a man and a father are Bishop Charles E. Blake, Bishop Benjamin Crouch, and Bishop G.E. Patterson. They helped mold and shape me to be the man I am today.

There was a gap growing up where I had no one. It was nothing but a miracle of God that, in the absence of a man, father and mentor, I did not go astray. I give God praise to this day. One thing I do know is when my father forsook me, God filled in the gap and became my Father and my mentor. Now that I'm much older and look back over my life, when I thought no one was there, God was there all the time. I give Him praise for that. What I'm saying is every young man has the ability to make right choices and right decisions. You've just got to make sure you do not allow your environment to influence your choices. Many young men are in prison today by the thousands. Not because someone made them do so, but because of decisions they made. I remember when God protected me from going to jail. God did that! I was working at a restaurant as Head Chef and the manager, an older lady, really took to me. She liked me and treated me like a son. One day she co-signed a car for me. We had a good relationship, but, eventually, I quit the job and started working for another company. One day I went outside, and the car was gone. She had it repossessed. Now, I was making the payments and wasn't behind, but she had to repossess it. I guess she did it because everything was in her name, and she could. As a young man, I didn't realize it at the time. I went to the restaurant where she worked and asked her what happened. She looked at me and said, *"Yes I've repossessed it."* I tell you I lost it! I ran and grabbed a big butcher knife out of the kitchen, pinned her against the wall and said, *"You're going to give me back my car."* At the time, I couldn't explain who it was, but now I know it was God who told me to put the knife down. I put it down and walked out of the restaurant. She never called the police; I was never arrested, and I was never charged. That was God!

Years later after I became a national gospel recording artist and record producer, I was in that city doing a radio interview. The radio station was interviewing me about a new song I just released called *God Is Faithful.* People could call in to the station and talk to me as the artist. A female caller was put through and she said, *"Hello Norman, don't you remember me?"* I couldn't believe it. This caller was the same lady from the restaurant who I had pinned against the wall. She continued, *"I have been following your career. I love your music and I'm very proud of you."* This was a White lady! I cried because I could have been a statistic. Think about it. A young Black man with a butcher knife in his hand pinning a White woman against the wall in Georgetown, DE where they still had the death penalty by hanging you by your neck in the Georgetown circle. God protected me and I give him praise! For every young man who will ever read this chapter, I want you to know that life is about choices and decisions. If you make choices and decisions based on your anger, resentment and pain, oftentimes, it leads to destruction. When you take a deep breath and think about the consequences, there's always a better way. Has to be. Got to be a better way.

I gave my heart to Christ when I was young, but I hadn't developed a mind to hear and listen to the Holy Spirit to lead and guide me. Still, God knew my heart and, oftentimes, He intervened when I would have made wrong choices and bad decisions. I believe He knew what He had in store for me, for my future, my purpose and my destiny. So, it's only by the grace of God that I am who I am. Not because I made all the right choices, not because I made all of the right decisions, but because, in my ignorance and my inability to think things through, God's grace was sufficient for me. His strength was made perfect in my weakness. One of the major things I've learned in life is never use as an excuse, "I didn't have anybody in my life, I didn't have a father, I didn't have a mentor, I didn't have a man." I didn't have anybody in my life. I didn't have a father, I didn't have a mentor, I didn't have a man. The truth of the matter is, the fact that you were born a man, God has already put inside you the ability to mature and become what He has created you to be. Nobody teaches an acorn to be an oak tree. It is innate. It is inside the seed and grows to become an oak tree. Not because it's been taught or trained. It was God-given that inside every boy is a man. God determined that. Here's a good question. Who was the example of a man for the first man Adam? How did Adam know how to be a husband? How did he know how to be a father? It is because God the Creator put that inside of him. Do not be influenced by the negativity of what you see around you. Look to God, pray and He will place positive, respectful men in your life that are not intimidated by who you are, your gifts and your talents. Then, when you have matured and become what God has purposed by design for you to be; to show your love and your gratitude to God, reach back and help some young men become that man, that father, that mentor. Help them to grow and develop, and become all that God has purposed and destined for their lives

Even after becoming an adult, God would place powerful men as mentors in my life. It was actually during that critical age between nine and fourteen years old that I had no one. Particularly after I discovered that my biological father was a pastor who disowned me as his son because he did not want people to know he had me out of wedlock. I was eight years old when I was licensed as a minister. At twelve it seemed pastors looked up to or gravitated to me, when I turned twelve, my mother told the pastor, *"He's yours now. I need you to take him under your wing, train him and raise him for me. I've done all I can do."* He did just that. It was confusing though, because one minute I thought he liked me and then the next minute I thought he didn't. He used to give me some very strange advice. Once I was on my way to a revival he had to preach. I was traveling with him as the musician playing the piano and organ. He said, *"Whenever you get married, if you cheat on your wife, don't tell her."* I thought to myself, *"Was that the best advice to give to a young boy?"* I was so puzzled. So many things he said to me were confusing. I believe if I had listened and made his opinions a part of who I was, I wouldn't have turned out to be who I am now. Trying to find the right examples and mentors was always difficult for me growing up as a young man.

Everybody in your circle has their own agendas, especially when you are gifted and talented. They can see, for the lack of a better word, dollar signs. The way they can capitalize on who you are, and it was easy to see. You get that feeling in your gut. I believe every young man needs mentors because they are a product of their environment. When all you see is negative things, they tend to chart a course for you. When you can see positive things, that can have a major impact on your life. One thing I am grateful and thankful for is never getting into any major trouble that altered my life and put me in the hands of the authorities. I was afraid of drugs and afraid of alcohol because I saw what it did to many of my brothers. Their lives were really messed up because of that. The truth of the matter is, I learned how to be a young man by watching other men from a distance. You could say I was a student of television. It is amazing the impact television can have on a young person. When I would see positive role models and the way they handled life and business and things, I began to emulate that. One of my most favorite TV dads was Andy Griffith from the *Andy Griffith Show* and his little son, Opie. Boy, did I admire their relationship. When Opie got in trouble, his father didn't abuse him and talk down to him, but he used the opportunity to teach him life lessons. So many times, I pretended I was Opie, and Andy Griffith was my father. I think I've seen just about every episode ever recorded. There is some truth to finding positive men and emulating them. One of the challenges many young men face is not having access to positive role models they can talk to or be in their presence to watch and learn from them. Oftentimes, I thought about what life would have been for me as a young boy if my biological father and I had a father-son relationship. No man has ever taken me fishing or hiking. No man has ever visited me at school or been to any of my basketball or football games. No man has come to see me in the school concerts. When I became a member of the choir, I used to watch other young boys in my school as their fathers would show up. Men would hug and embrace their boys, and I overheard conversations about how proud they were of them. What was so amazing is even though I did not have that camaraderie, and I can't explain it but, somehow I would reach way down inside of me and become my own best friend. You may think I'm crazy, but there were times when I looked at myself in the mirror and talked to my reflection as if I was my own father. I would say to myself, *"I'm proud of you. You're doing a great job!"* I would even fuss at myself when I knew I did something wrong or wasn't doing things I should do. I really would. If someone walked in and saw me fussing at myself, they probably would suggest I be committed as soon as possible. I did like David did. In the Bible it says he encouraged himself. Because I was growing up as a young preacher who knew and studied the Bible and practiced following the commandments of God, I submitted myself. So when I did do wrong, I didn't go to the extreme because, the truth is, conviction is real. If I told a lie or as a kid would steal something I would feel so convicted by my actions. There was one pastor I sat under for several years. We all knew something was wrong with him, but we couldn't quite put our hands on it. Later, we discovered he was an alcoholic. What an example for a young ten-year-old preacher. I mean there were times when he could barely stand up. Once he came by the house, for what reason I do not know, but he was drunk. We made him go in the house, took him in a bedroom and let him lay down to sleep it off. He slept for a long time. It was in the middle of the day during the summer when we were out of school. After a few hours he woke up and decided to leave. Backing out of the driveway he hit the mailbox, so he wasn't quite normal again all the way. In the mind of a young preacher, you begin asking yourself, *"Is this the way it's supposed to be?"* There was something deep inside me, even as young as I was, that felt it was wrong and not the way to live. Later in life, God would place powerful men around me to be my mentors. I gleaned from them and learned the things I should do. I thank God, in spite of all the negativity I saw and experienced, I never desired to do what they did. At the end of the day, it is all about choices. No matter how young you are you can still make the right choice.

Mothers Raising Boys

For single mothers who are raising young boys in this day and time; in the climate in which we live, not to mention all the things we are exposed to through social media and so many different outlets, it is so important, and critical that God has a single mother. You still need to find someone to be a mentor to your young men. I know it's difficult. It's not easy, but the best place to start is a seasoned church with a young men's ministry. This will become a foundation that not only teaches them about spirituality, but also promotes life principles that will teach them to be honorable and respectful. One thing every young man needs growing up is to be accountable to someone. There are so many different thoughts that enter your mind and so many different options and temptations. Because of lack of maturity, and not thinking about consequences in years to come, oftentimes, young men make decisions based on gratification in the moment. A wrong choice today can affect your life, long term. When you have a mentor, someone you trust, a man's man, you establish a rapport with him to build a relationship. Young men will receive constructive criticism from someone they love and trust. Even then there's a right way and a wrong way to approach young men. At the age I am now and having experienced growing up in the 60s, 70s and 80s without a father, I have had powerful mentors throughout my life. I, too, have become a mentor to other young men across the country. It wasn't something I asked for. When you meet young men and they spend time in your presence, it doesn't take long for them to discern who you are. I've had them ask me to be their mentor or if they could call me Pops. At first I didn't want to embrace it. I really didn't. But I grew, and now I have young sons all across the country that I mentor and speak into their lives. They trust the wisdom life and God has given me down through the years, and I'm honored. Every young man needs a mirror, a reflection of themselves: someone who's been there, done that and got the T-Shirt. As a mentor you need to be honest with them, then teach and show them what to expect out of life. Not only that, but one thing I've learned is it's difficult to accept constructive criticism or even advice from someone who has not succeeded at anything. One of my pet peeves is never go to someone for advice who has only failed at what you are trying to succeed at in life. They do not have a story or testimony of victory. All they will do is rehearse their defeat. You must find someone who has succeeded at what they started going after in life. It may not exactly be the road you want to travel, but many of the principles are still the same. Listen to how they succeeded, some of the trials and mistakes they've made. What are the things they did to bounce back when life threw a curve? What do they do when it seems like the bottom has been pulled out from under them? How did they bounce back from a fall? Yes, it takes someone who has failed and succeeded. They make great mentors! I remember one young man I was mentoring who was in the Foster care system. He had a very difficult time developing in life and I did my best to help him. Eventually I had to separate myself from him because, sometimes, people are just so traumatized by life you can't save them. You can't save everybody. I was always the type of person who would not to be defeated by challenges. You have to know and recognize when you've done all you can do. If you don't learn from a mentor, life will teach you, and you might not like the end result.

We can't give up on our young men! We have to do all we can to help them. I know sometimes it doesn't seem like we are making a difference. If we can just help one, if we can steer just one away from prison and trouble, we can make a difference. There was a story that was told about a young boy who was on the beach throwing starfish back in the ocean that had floated onto the shore. There were hundreds of them. A lady passed by and saw what the young man was doing and asked, *"What are you doing?"* He said, *"I'm throwing the starfish back in the ocean."* She looked at the hundreds of starfish on the beach and said, *"There are too many for you to make a difference."* The little boy didn't say anything. He just reached down and picked up another starfish and threw it in the ocean. Then he said to the lady, *"Tell it to that one."* We may not be able to save everybody, but tell it to that one. There's a song we used to sing years ago in church called, *If I Can Help Somebody.* A piece of the verse says, *"If I can help somebody as I pass along then my living will not be in vain."* We can't be so busy at life and pursuing our own dreams that we do not reach back and help some other young man.

I was fortunate growing up as a young boy. I can't even explain it, but it just wasn't in me to go down the wrong path. I don't know where I learned it from. All I know is I wanted more. I just wanted more. I never was the kind of person to become so angry at life I wanted to make other people pay for or feel my pain. I was always the kind of young fella who made the best out of everything. I think one of the secrets to success or becoming a strong productive young man is to find the goals or dream and go after it. Let that become the driving force of your life. I believe that's what happened to me. My dream and desires of who I wanted to be when I grew up consumed me day in and day out. I was always doing something. I was playing with the toys of my future, who I would become. Now when I look back over my life at sixty-two years young, not only am I living my dream, but I'm still dreaming dreams. As long as there is life, there's always something to pursue. Get a dream, get a vision, and go after it!

One of the most dangerous things in life, and a serious caution, is to be careful how life fills the void of what you do not have. I remember standing at the graveside of my biological father who disowned me as his son, thinking I will never get to know him, and he will never get to know me. But because I forgave him, I walked away with a clean heart. I haven't been back to his grave since because I have no memories. I don't know what color he likes or what his favorite foods are. I don't know some of the challenges he faced growing up as a young man. I've never had a father to say I'm proud of you. I've never had a father to say I love you. Life has a way of filling the void. The challenge is you've got to be careful to make sure it is positive and not negative. Forgiveness helps you to fight bitterness, anger and resentment. You did not have what you felt you needed growing up, but for me I can honestly say the hand of God was on my life. He protected and provided for me and kept me from hurt, harm and danger. Even though I've experienced some major challenges in my life, which we will talk about in the next chapter. In spite of it all, I'm alive. Everything I needed from a man I have today because God placed men, spiritual fathers, spiritual mentors in my life. The craziest thing about it is I did not seek them out. God put them in my path because of the promise He made to me the day of my biological father's funeral. On the porch, looking out across the field at his grave, God said to me, *"I will place men in your life to father you, to mentor you, to teach you, and to train you."* It wasn't many years later God began to guide my path. The steps of a good man are ordered by the Lord, and He began to lead and guide me. Now I have the wisdom, the experience, the knowledge of three men I call giants in the faith. Moses is of the faith who have sown into me as a Joshua. Now my only goal and desire is to help other young men become a man's man.

God is doing for me now what he did for me back then, putting young men in my path. All I'm doing is emulating what I've experienced. I want to end this chapter by saying to any single mother who is raising young men, I know you're doing the best you can. What you didn't know is I'm proud of you. You didn't ask to be a mother and father; it just happens to be that way. But my prayer for you is that God will put in your path positive role models and mentors that can help your young man become all that God has purposed and destined for his life. It's a long road, it's a long journey, but trust in God. Having faith in God, He will lead you and guide you in the right direction. I am who I am today because of the sum total of men, good men, God has placed in my life. As an act of gratitude, I will do all I can to help every starfish, if you know what I mean.

CHAPTER TWELVE

LIVING THROUGH MIRACLES

The Book of Psalm, Chapter 121 says, *"I will lift up my eyes unto the hills from whence cometh my help my help coming from the Lord."* Then in Matthew Chapter 5, it says, *"He sendeth rain on the just as well as the unjust."* Just because we are Believers and followers of Christ, does not exempt us from trouble, trial and adversity. As a matter of fact, Jesus said, *"If any man will come after me, let him deny himself, take up his cross and follow me."* I have always said, no matter what life throws at you, my conviction is this, God will do one of two things. He will deliver you from it or give you the grace to go through it. Either way is victory. When I look back over my life and see all of the things that God has brought me through, I see His hand has always been on my life. I remember one time I was complaining to God about some of the situations I was going through. The Holy Spirit said to me, *"You're complaining about what you've been through, but you're not thanking Me for what you have survived."* God has brought me through a long, winding road, but I've seen miracle after miracle after miracle. This is my testimony of healing and deliverance and seeing the power of God at work in my life.

Going Blind

It was the winter of 2005. My wife and I were living in Dover, Delaware pastoring the church we both founded together, Frontline Ministries. We were also very busy touring across the country doing concerts and preaching engagements. One morning I woke up and everything visually looked crooked. I was walking straight but everything was crooked, even the lines on the road. I saw double vision, like two of everything. I told my wife about it, and we decided to go get my vision checked. After the doctor reviewed the tests he said, *"You're going blind, and you need a surgery."* I remember saying to him, *"I have to go out of town to do a concert and when I get back, we'll do that."* He said, *"You do not understand. If you leave and go out of town, by the time you get back you will be blind. You need an emergency surgery right now."* The very next day we went to Salisbury, Maryland to a hospital where they prepped me for surgery. As they were rolling me down the hallway, I could hear music that was very familiar as we got closer to the operating room. Somehow, they found out I was a recording artist and decided they would play my music during the surgery. Out of all of the songs I've written, the song I heard playing was *Nobody But You*. The lyrics say, *"Nobody but you Lord, nobody but you. When I was in trouble you came to my rescue, Nobody but you Lord, nobody but you."* As I lay there, they told me they would put me in what is called twilight sleep. Which meant, I may wake up but I wouldn't be able to feel anything or see anything. I remember waking up midway through the surgery and could see the instruments they were using to operate on my eyes. I remember it looking like Star Wars. They discovered that the retinas in both eyes were detaching due to complications from diabetes. Diabetes runs very deeply in my family. My father, my mother and many of my sisters and brothers had diabetes. I believe I had it as a child but wasn't diagnosed. After I became a young man and was told I had the disease, I remembered having symptoms while I was in fifth grade. I dozed back off to sleep during the surgery. When I woke up in the recovery room, I was completely blind. I could not see! The doctors told me they did all they could do to reconnect my retinas. One of them was totally lost. They said I would be blind in one eye and there was no way to repair it. They were able to reconnect the retina in the other eye but, unfortunately, I was blind because the blood vessels in the back of the eye burst. No one can see through blood. The doctors were hopeful the eye would heal, and I would at least be able to see out of one.

I remember being at home preparing to meet with the church deacons to share the news that I was blind. We met at the administrative office in the conference room. The deacons were sitting in the conference room before I came in. When everyone arrived and got settled, my wife led me to the conference room. When I walked in all I could hear, because

I could not see, is them saying things like, *"Oh my God what is wrong with pastor?He's blind, he can't see!"* I even heard one of the deacons crying. I began explaining what happened and that I wanted to meet with them at the church. I wanted them to practice with me walking down the aisle and counting the steps leading up to the pulpit.

Because I was determined to continue preaching, my wife would read scriptures to me, and I would record them in my studio. By Sunday, I would have memorized them. The first day I went to church blind, it was packed to capacity. I was told when I walked out of the office and down the aisle, as they were leading me, I could hear people in the congregation. Many of them were crying, many of them were saying things like, *"Oh, my God, is pastor blind?"* When it was time for me to preach, I had already practiced sitting on the front row and counting the steps to the first step that led to the top, which was really only three steps. I faced the audience from the pulpit but could not see them. I explained that because of the complications of diabetes, my retinas were detached. I never shared with them that I was already half blind and believing God the other eye would heal, and I would see out of that eye. I stood there and preached my heart out, then we went home.

People don't understand that going blind is one thing and dealing with mental capacity is another thing. Will I ever see again? Was this the way it was going to be for the rest of my life? The thing that built my faith and kept me believing is God was my music and my devotional time in worship. When I sat at my piano in my studio I could play for hours! I even went to the office and learned how to operate my telephone. I still made phone calls and did new member interviews. Even when my wife cooked for me, I would sit in the family room where she would set up the tray and say, *"Your broccoli is at 12:00, your rice is at 3:00, your baked chicken is at 3:45,"* on the plate. I learned my way around the house which was my safety zone.

Other than Sundays, I wouldn't go out unless I was going to the office. One time my wife said, *"I wanna take you to the store."* I was so afraid, but she had a plan. We went to Target, and she said to me, *"You hold onto the back of the cart. I'll get in the front, and you just follow the cart."* She led me throughout the store buying items, and I felt like everybody was watching me. We really didn't run into anybody we knew personally. When it came to feeling like a man who wanted to protect his wife in the event of harm or danger, I felt so helpless. My safety zone was in the house. Week after week went by with no progress. I would preach every Sunday, and it got to a point where I would preach and lose my direction. Sometimes they had to come up and get me and say, *"Pastor we're this way not that way."* I was facing the wall and not the congregation, but that's where I found the most peace. That's where I felt my best even though I was blind.

We would go to the doctor to get my eyes checked. I remember him saying, *"You have to stop preaching so hard because it's not helping your eyes. You are making it worse."* I told him, *"I'm just a Pentecostal preacher and that's the way we preach."* He said, *"Yeah, but if you want to get better, just talk to the people. You don't have to raise your voice."* That's just like telling someone you can't breathe! We had a second surgery with no success. The ride home was long and quiet, but my wife started talking faith and belief in God! She told me this is not how my story ends. One morning I woke up and heard my wife getting dressed. It had snowed about four to five inches, and I asked her, *"What are you doing?"* She said, *"I'm getting dressed to go outside to shovel the snow off of our walkway and the driveway."* The man in me stood up and she said, *"What are you doing?"* I said, *"I'm getting dressed, too."* She asked why and I said, *"I'm going to shovel the snow with you."*

A Blind Man Shoveling Snow

Interesting, right? A blind man shoveling snow. She didn't discourage me. So, I got dressed, and she helped me walk outside. I said, *"Give me a shovel."* She gave me a shovel, and I asked her to point me to where the snow was. She did and, even though I couldn't see it, I felt good as a man to shovel the snow. I didn't realize at the time I was shoveling the snow in a spot she had already cleared. We laughed and it was probably the first time I'd really laughed since becoming blind.

People were visiting the church because they heard Norman Hutchins, the preacher, the recording artist, was blind. It got to a point where people were joining the church and still giving their heart to Jesus. I started saying, *"Stick around, I'll see you again one day."* Like David, I began to encourage myself in the Lord. We had another surgery, and this would be the third one. The doctors were very hopeful and even suggested after this surgery I should be able to see again. We stayed in the hotel next door to the hospital that night in preparation for the surgery the next day. My wife and I stayed up all night long singing, playing music and praying. She held me and spoke into my life. Early that morning I had surgery. When I woke up, I had blinds on both my eyes. It was frightening because I didn't know there was a difference between white blindness and black blindness. The best way to describe white blindness would be like looking up at the sky and the clouds. Black blindness would be like the dark sky at nighttime. Even though it would only be one day before they would take the blinds off my eyes, hopefully by then I would be able to see. I couldn't wait! Like I said, at that moment I felt like white blindness would be better than black blindness if I had to be blind for the rest of my life. The following day we went to the doctor's office, with fingers crossed, prepared to take the blinds off my eyes, hoping I would be able to see. When he took the blinds off, I could see my wife. I hadn't seen her in three months, but now she looked like she was about five hundred feet away even though she was standing next to me. After two minutes I couldn't see again; something to do with the blood and the vessels and the one eye. I was already totally blind in one eye. I said to the doctor, *"We've had three surgeries with no success. Just be honest with me, will I ever see again? I was hoping for the best but preparing for the worst. Do I have to start making adjustments to live like this for the rest of my life?"* Unexpectedly, the answer the doctor gave me shook me to the core. He said, *"You are a pastor. Don't you believe in miracles?"* When he said that my faith was rejuvenated.

On the long drive back to Dover, DE which was a little over an hour and fifteen minutes, we began to believe God for a miracle. Usually, people who go blind from complications of diabetes never see again, but we were believing God. When I preached every Sunday, I always concluded with, *"I'll see you again."* By telling the congregation I would see them again, my faith began to increase. I preached to myself. Something strange started happening. While I was blind, my spiritual sight increased. Because I couldn't see physically, my spiritual side allowed me to experience, see and hear things without any distractions from the physical sight. There's a verse in the Bible that says, *"While we look not at the things that are seen but at the things that are not seen for the things that are seen are temporal but the things that are not seen are eternal."* Sometimes what we see in the physical can affect our faith spiritually. Because I could not see, I had no choice but to trust God.

I remember one morning my wife got up and said she was going to the office. I decided to stay home. When she left, I went into my studio, sat there and began singing to God and writing music. As a matter of fact, some of the most popular songs I've written were while I was blind. The songs, *Where I Long To Be, A Move of God is On The Way, When I Wake Up In The Morning,* just to name a few, were written while I was blind. In fact, I did a live recording in Los Angeles at Maranatha totally blind. That particular day, while I was in my studio just singing to God, all of a sudden, the room became brighter than I'd ever seen. It was a sun porch so I could almost tell the time of the day based on the brightness of the room. But this particular day it was brighter than I'd ever seen it. All of a sudden it felt like somebody was in the house. I screamed out, *"Who's in the house! Who's in this house!"* but nobody answered. The room got bright and all of a sudden, joy and a peace came over me that I can't even explain. I started asking God, *"What is this? What is this feeling?"* The Holy Spirit responded saying, *"I'm giving you a glimpse of glory."* I replied to God saying, *"If I never see you again, if I can just feel what I feel right now I'll be okay."*

Weeks passed and I'm now in a routine. Wake up in the morning, eat breakfast, go to the office, teach bible study, prepare for Sunday, go and preach. I didn't travel, I didn't do concerts, I didn't do speaking engagements. Everything I did revolved solely around church. The last Sunday I preached blind was unusual. The power of God fell in the house as I preached from the subject, "This Is Not How My Story Ends". The Lord anointed me to preach that sermon that day, and towards the end of the service the Holy Spirit spoke to me. He said, *"Because of your faithfulness and because of the assignment I have for your life, today is the last day anybody will lead you down this aisle."* I even shared it with the congregation. I was so excited! I went home. Monday, Tuesday, no vision. Wednesday, Thursday, no vision. At the top of the week my faith was at 100%. By midweek I think it was at 50% because I thought God would have given me my sight back by then. Now we are at Saturday so I'm thinking to myself, maybe I need to stay home an extra week, you know, to help God out. I had told the church the Lord said this would be the last Sunday anyone would lead me down the aisle. How can I go to church Sunday, which would be tomorrow and still have to hold on to someone's shoulder walking down the aisle? Did God really tell me that? Did the Holy Spirit say that, or was it wishful thinking? I do remember making up my mind that I would not stay home, but I would still go to church and preach. Saturday night I got ready for bed and in my prayer, I prayed and quoted the verse of a song that I wrote, it says, "*If God said it that settles it and that's good enough for me,*" and I went to bed. I can't remember exactly what time it was but early in the morning, just before dawn, I woke up and something unusual happened.

Wake Up, I Can See

I looked over at my wife and I could see her silhouette. I got closer to her while she was asleep and could see the shape of her nose. I woke her up! "*Honey, morning, wake up, wake up, I can see you! I can see you!*" I mean I had to get close, as close as my hand touching my nose, but I could see her, and I could see her silhouette. She jumps up and we just start praising and thanking God! I could see the shape of the bed, I could see the shape of the dresser, I could see the doorway leading out into the hallway, but just the shadows. We got up later that morning and got dressed. This would be the day! When we arrived at the church, as always, the deacons greeted me at the car and led me. When they opened the door I said, "*I got this.*" I couldn't tell who was who. I could only see their shadows. When service time started the church was packed out. I walked down the aisle by myself without holding on to anybody just like God said. I'm telling you that was a miracle service because they saw me from the beginning, and they were seeing God's Word come to pass. From that day forward, every day, my vision got better and better and better. In less than thirty days I could see again. I knew everybody, I could see everybody. Then I prayed and told God I wanted to drive again.

When I went to my doctor's appointment, he asked me to read the smallest line on the eye chart. I couldn't see the big "E" but I kept pulling them back and about the third time, I saw the qualifying line below the line. That was twenty years ago, and I can still see. No, I did not get 100% of my vision back but, the truth of the matter is, it was good for me. Anytime I want to feel what I felt when I couldn't see, all I have to do is close one eye. Doing that keeps me humble and in a spirit of gratitude. I promised God that if He would let me see again I would totally surrender and dedicate the rest of my life. Not just serving Him but being His voice,

His mouthpiece, to teach men and women His law. Some people may hear this and feel it is not a miracle I can see again but, I tell you what, I wouldn't trade places with this body for anyone else's on the face of this earth.

The Bible says, "*The sufferings of this present time are not worthy to be compared with the glory that shall be revealed in us.*" God gave me a miracle! To this day, the doctors don't understand why I'm not 100% blind. I'm not trying to understand it, I'm just giving glory and honor to God for allowing me to see His beautiful creation. I remember the first time I looked up into the sky and could see the blue, I can see a cloud. I remember when I looked in the front yard and I could see the yellow flowers, I wrote a song that says, "*When I wake up in the morning and see the bright sunshine I will lift my hands toward heaven and thank Him for another day, another day, another day, eyes to see, ears to hear, legs to walk and a voice to talk, another day, another day, thank you, Lord, for another day.*"

As I mentioned in the beginning of this chapter, the Bible says, "*He sendeth rain on the just as well as the unjust,*" and just because you are a Believer in Christ does not exempt you from trouble, trial and adversity. We have to learn, as Believers, to endure hardship as good soldiers. Again, God will do one of two things. He will either deliver us from it or give us the grace to go through it. In difficult times it is our faith that should stand strong. The Bible says, "*So faith without works is dead,*" and it also says, "*whose report will you believe?*" One of the greatest lessons I've learned in walking with God is that His silence is not His absence. Sometimes you can pray and seemingly get no answer, but God is working behind the scenes doing and positioning things you have no idea. No matter what life throws your way, do not let God pay the price for your sufferings. I will trust in the Lord no matter what I face. Faith is the foundation of your belief system. You do not just trust God when everything is going well, but you trust God when the bottom falls out. I have learned the same praise in your valley is the same praise you've got to demonstrate on your mountain. God doesn't always deliver us from the valley because, when He eventually gives us the mountain, the same praise in the valley is the same praise on top of the mountain.

One of the greatest challenges of my life happened in 2015. I woke up one morning and I was feeling totally different and couldn't explain it. My wife and I got dressed to go to church on a Sunday morning. While in the office before I went out to preach, I started feeling worse but, as always, I pushed myself. When I started preaching, I told myself I better make this sermon short because I really do not feel like I'm gonna make it. No sooner than I had that thought, I vomited right in front of hundreds of people at Frontline Ministries, the church I was pastoring. I went to sit down, and some dutiful staff members attended to me as one of the elders stood to finish the service. Upon going to the doctor, it was discovered I had renal failure. My kidneys were bad, and I had to undergo emergency surgery to have a port inserted in my neck. They were prepping me for dialysis. I'm sitting there trying to understand how in the world I got to this point. Dialysis was certainly not part of my dream. It was not in line with the vision God had been giving me about my destiny, my future and things He wanted me to do for Him. I remember the first day of dialysis. It was on January 8, 2015. I was so afraid and very quiet. I really didn't have much conversation with people when I walked into the dialysis center. I was greeted and the nurses were very friendly. I sat in the chair, and they began connecting me to the dialyzing machine. Now I'm looking at my blood coming from my body. It circles throughout these tubes and goes inside of the dialyzer. Once it is cleansed, they put it back in my body. This process took almost five hours. It was so difficult to understand how I got to this point. I'm looking around at all of the other patients and thinking to myself, God help me! The enemy started talking to me and I remember him saying, *"So you've been preaching since you were how old, eight years old, and this is how God shows you love?"* I didn't respond, then I heard the enemy say, *"This is where you are going to die."* All I could do was sit there and pray; I was so afraid. When it was over they disconnected me from the machine, and I went home. The first night after dialysis I couldn't sleep because of the way it made my body feel. That was on Monday. Tuesday was my day off. By the time I had recuperated on Tuesday, it was time to go back to dialysis on Wednesday. We would repeat the process Monday, Wednesday and Friday. After my first week, I got frustrated hearing the enemy speaking negative things to my spirit. So, finally, I spoke up and said, *"Devil, you will never convince me that the God I've been serving all of these years is going to leave me in the shape that I'm in."* I told the enemy, *"I'm believing God for a miracle,"* and I also said, *"God is going to do one of two things, either He's going to deliver me from it or give me the grace to go through it."* I created my pattern for the day when I went to dialysis starting with prayer. I would read the Bible then listen to gospel music and wrote several songs while I was being dialyzed. Last, I remember one of the worst days in dialysis. I felt anxiety and a spirit of depression preventing me from doing all the things I was doing before I started dialysis.

I was traveling every week, pretty much, preaching and doing concerts all across the country when it all came to a halt. When I preached on Sundays, I would tell the church I was believing God for a miracle. All of a sudden, something strange happened. Thirty people in the church stood up and said, *"Pastor, we would like to be tested to see if we are a match for you to get a kidney transplant."* I couldn't believe it! When I went to my doctor's office to let them know we had people interested in being tested, they said because of my health, my heart, and all of the other challenges I was facing, I didn't qualify for a transplant. I'm thinking, *"God, are you telling me that thirty people in my church have stood to be tested and the doctors are telling me I do not qualify? How much worse can it get?"* I've learned from scripture that sometimes you have to hope against hope when things really seem hopeless. You have got to stand on the Word of God. What kept my faith strong was the fact I was still preaching every Sunday morning and teaching Bible study every Tuesday night. The same messages and teachings I was sharing with the congregation, I also received for myself. Ultimately, the doctor said, *"Well, go to dialysis for three months and we will test you again to see if you've gotten any better. Then we may consider testing the people who have stood."* I faithfully went to dialysis, and it got to a point where the nurses knew what time of day it was based on what I was doing. I was preparing myself spiritually and doing spiritual warfare. I was believing God for a miracle. One day, I felt so down and discouraged, like your faith being on a roller coaster. It's up one day and the next day it's down. Then there was physical pain and cramping in my legs which was almost unbearable. There is an unexplainable sick feeling in your stomach and a fatigue that comes with dialysis. I don't even know what to say. It's just, you can't function, you can't think. You have to push your way through it. One time, I went outside after dialysis and was so down. A good friend of mine left a note on my truck. To this day, he will never know how that note encouraged me. I got in the truck and, as I always did, I didn't go home and go to bed. I went to the office and worked. I still did premarital counseling and my daily administrative duties as a pastor. After one of my dialysis sessions, the enemy started talking again, telling me, *"You will never qualify for kidney transplant,"* or *"Things are just going get worse for you."* I talked back to the enemy, *"Satan, you see this lady next to me? She's on dialysis. Why does she have no legs? But I got legs, and when I finish here, I'm going to walk out of here."* I saw them bring another man in on a gurney. I said, *"See this man they brought in on a gurney? When I finish, I'm going to walk up out of here!"* Every negative thing the enemy tried to throw at me, I responded with my faith. How about two months into dialysis, the Holy Spirit said to me, *"You will not be on dialysis more than six months."* I know the Holy Spirit when I hear Him because He's spoken to me before. I knew He meant it but here comes the enemy. He said, *"So you think you're gonna just come in here? You have people here that's been on dialysis for five, ten, fifteen years. We had just celebrated a lady who had been on dialysis almost twenty years and you're gonna get out in six months?"* I said to the enemy, *"If God said it I believe it and you can't make me doubt it. God said six months!"*

One in 2.5 Million

Four months in, we went to dinner, my wife and me. After dinner, my wife says to me, *"I have some news for you."* I said, *"What is it?"* She said, *"I secretly went and got tested."* I was like, *"Ohh, no, no, no, you can't do that."* Then she said, *"And, I found out that I am a perfect match."* WOW! The surgeon said she was one in 2.5 million! You know, my wife is from the islands, Belize, Central America. It was so amazing my wife would be a perfect match. We told the doctors when I went for my next examination. We were praying all the way, nervous but trusting God. When I sat on the bed two doctors came in and they were examining me and asking all kinds of questions. As I looked at their eyes and listened to their comments, things didn't sound favorable. It didn't seem like they were going to approve me to be tested for the transplant. I told God, *"My wife is a perfect match. Please let it happen."* One of the doctors said, *"Well, we're going to get the chief surgeon who would be the one to perform the surgery."* He came into the room and started examining me and asking questions. As he was poking throughout my body with such a blank face, I didn't know if the outcome would be positive or negative. Finally, after about ten minutes he patted me on my shoulder and said to the other doctors, my wife and me, *"Let's get him transplanted!"* My God! You're talking about the joy of the Lord that filled that room! We were in Philadelphia at the University of Pennsylvania. My wife and I praised God all the way back home, but we were facing another challenge. My wife and I did not have insurance for both surgeries. My surgery was more $300,000, and my wife's was over $300,000, but we were trusting God. Finally, God opened a major door! My wife and I qualified for a program, I don't even know how to this day. It paid 100% of my surgery and my wife's surgery. The surgery was scheduled for June 8th, six months, just like God said. On my last day of dialysis, I was saying goodbye to all of the constituents, nurses and the people I had come to know. It was bittersweet, though, as during the second half of the day I started running a high fever. My blood was clogging up the machine, so they had to take me off of dialysis for about an hour. I mean, everything that could go wrong went wrong that day. Finally, I was excited when the day was over because it was my last day at dialysis and the very next day would be my transplant surgery. When I got outside, I turned around and took a picture of the building. I went to my car and, before I could unlock the door, my phone rang. It was my wife. By the sound of her voice, I could tell something was wrong. "*What is it?*" I asked. She said they cancelled the surgery. I felt like someone had punched me in my chest! Apparently, one of the dialysis nurses called the doctor and told them how bad my day was. I couldn't believe it! Why would she do such a thing? I hung up the phone and got in my car. I sat there for a moment not saying a word thinking, I do remember telling God, *"I don't believe You would let my wife be a perfect match and the surgery not happen."* Ask God what's going on. All of a sudden, the Holy Spirit said to me, *"It is delayed but not denied."*I began to rejoice and then I went home. What I'm thinking now is I have to go back to dialysis. When I walked in the dialysis room, knowing we celebrated me leaving, taking pictures and all that, I knew it was going to be terrible for me. Sure enough, when I walked in on Wednesday, *"What happened?"* was the biggest question of the day! *"What happened? I thought the other day was your last day!"* I mean one after another, after another, questions were asked, but I made it through the day. Finally, the surgery was rescheduled. The day before the surgery I met with the doctor who would be the chief surgeon. I was in his office when he said, *"You know you're going to be* *the worst patient I've ever operated on."* Then he said, *"I suspect you might die during the surgery."* I'm sitting there listening and then he said, *"We'll have a team prepared, you know, to do all that we can. I have to tell you these things so that you know what the risks are."* Then he walked out of the room and left me there by myself. I guess to think about what he said, I had a conversation with God, I said, *"Lord, I do not believe You would let my wife be a perfect match, one in 2.5 million, and me not go through this surgery."* I said, *"Lord, this is what we're going to do. We're gonna go through with it and one of two things is going to happen; either I'm going to survive it or I'm going to wake up in heaven with You."* So, when the doctor came back in, he said, *"So what do you think?"* I said, *"Let's do it!"*

On the day of the surgery, we're at the University of Pennsylvania. They're prepping my wife first; I'm sitting next to her by her bed filled with emotions. At this time, we've been married almost twenty years, trying to figure out how in the world can someone love someone this much. She was, I could see it in her eyes, so afraid, but she wouldn't say it. She was very nervous but was doing it for love. I kissed her and we prayed together, then they rolled her into the operating room. Next, they called my name, *"It's time for you to be prepped."* The surgery would take place in two operating rooms that were next door to each other, so when they took the kidney out of my wife, they could just go next door and put her kidney in me. So now they're prepping me. I remember them pushing me down the hall. The anesthesiologist was prepared to put me to sleep. The next thing I knew the surgery was over and they rolled both of us into a recovery room. I looked over at my wife and she looked at me. The surgery was a success! They said as soon as they put the kidney in, it started working. My wife and I joined hands, and we began to praise and thank God for what He had just done. As I laid on the bed I looked over at my wife. She is such a prissy young lady, so much so the first thing I noticed was she still had her earrings on. Apparently, she must have asked for them after she came out of surgery because I know you can't wear them inside the operating room. So, she had her earrings on, looking beautiful as ever. She just stared into my eyes, and I was so overwhelmed with gratitude, love and appreciation that my wife was willing to make that sacrifice for me. They rolled her out of the recovery area and took her to her room.

I Flatlined and Died

When she was gone, all of a sudden, I got sick and started vomiting really badly. There was a smell I can't explain other than it smelled like death. If you ask me, the doctor said they put a little more fluid in the kidney than they should have. I guess it was leaking into my lungs. When they did an X-ray, they discovered my lungs were 90% full. So I was drowning in the fluid. The doctors told me they had to drain that fluid out of my lungs, but they were going to put a tube in my throat to help me breathe. That's the last thing I remember before I flat lined and died. I was told my sisters were crying. One of my sisters even took a picture of me while I was dead and sent it to my niece in Germany. The surgeon went upstairs to tell my wife, *"I'm sorry, we lost your husband."* She sat up in the bed and said, *"He can't die! God is not finished with him yet!"* They must have thought she was delusional as she was in so much pain because of the kind of surgery she had. But through her pain she told the nurse, *"Put me in a wheelchair and take me to his room!"* On her way to my room, my wife says the Holy Spirit spoke to her and said, *"Pray for him but do not look at his face."* When she entered my room, she also said, *"If there's anyone in here that cannot believe God and trust God for a miracle, get out of the room."* Sad to say, my family left the room. My wife prayed for me just as He instructed her. The nurse said, *"We have a light pulse."* God brought me back to life and, after several hours, I woke up. They asked me my name, I knew it. They asked me where I was. I knew it. Someone asked me how long I was dead. I told them if I knew that, I wouldn't be dead. Apparently, I was not in my body for quite a while. On a Tuesday God brought me back to life. I went home Saturday, and we went to church that Sunday, and we praised and glorified God for his miracle working power. The first thing I thought about was what the doctor said in that room with me and him by ourselves. After thinking about it, what that doctor said was right. He was 100% right. He said he suspected I would die, and that's exactly what happened. I died. But what the doctor did not tell me was that God would bring me back to life again! Hallelujah! Hallelujah! Someone asked me what I saw while I was dead. I remember seeing my mother's face. Mom died in 1985. I saw her face briefly and several others. They were all old but looked healthy. My mother had that look on her face, that I remember growing up as a child, when I got in trouble. She never said a word, but the way she looked seemed as if she was saying, *"You can't come here."* I also remember several other things I saw and heard many days after God brought me back to life. While thinking in my bed about what I saw, the Holy Spirit said, *"I did not show you what you saw to talk about, but it was for you personally."*

I can say I do not need faith to believe in the existence of God any longer because, while I was dead, I had an encounter with Him. What I can tell you is, in the few days I was in the hospital before I was discharged, I saw two giants at my door at night. I can't explain it, but they were dressed in military uniforms and were so tall that their heads almost touched the ceiling in my room. I've never seen anything like it in any branch of our military. Their faces were covered, their backs were toward me and I asked God, *"Who are these?"* He responded by saying, *"These are angels. They are here to protect you from the forces of the enemy."* Many people do not believe in spiritual or supernatural events. Everyone has a different story of death, but I can say this. What I saw was so real and has left such a deep impression on my heart, and I will always trust God! I will be a testimony and a witness to the miracle working power of God. It's been ten years now since my transplant with no complications and no setbacks. To God be the glory! The Lord did leave an impression on my heart while I was dead. He left me a message a couple days after I came back to life.

You Cannot Live Bad Enough for God to Hate You

The message He left on my heart was also met with a commandment. He commanded me to tell it everywhere I go. He also said, *"You cannot live bad enough for God to ever hate you and you cannot live good enough for God to love you anymore than He already does."* You are his creation, and He loves you. I've been sharing that message of love all across this nation and around this world. You do not earn God's love, you do not have to work for God's love, you do not have to get His approval because, no matter who you are or where you're from, no matter what you've done, God loves you. The Bible says, *"God commanded His love toward us and that while we were, yet sinners Christ died for us."* God allowed me to live! He gave me back my freedom to travel, to preach, to teach and do concerts. I'm grateful! Thank you, God, for my wife, thank you for the miracle.

Finally, I will say to you who are listening and reading. Never give up on God no matter where you are in life, no matter what you're dealing with, no matter what you're going through. You have got to trust the miracle working power of God. I died but God brought me back to life and now I have two birthdays. My first birthday is the day my mother birthed me, September 27, 1962 and my second birthday is June 14, 2015. Happy birthday to me, happy birthday to me, happy birthday dear Norman, happy birthday to me! I have committed my life for the rest of my life to be an ambassador for God, to spread His word, His gospel, His message to encourage people. No matter where you are in life, *look to the hills from whence cometh your help.* God has not forsaken you nor has He forgotten you. You've got to endure hardness as a good soldier. Faith that is not tested cannot be trusted.

In 2021, America was hit with one of the worst pandemics I had ever experienced in my lifetime. It was COVID. From the beginning no one knew what it was, but eventually we found out. The first thing I remember as a pastor, we had to shut our church down. I couldn't believe that all of the churches across the nation and around the world were actually shut down. We started streaming live. I'm sitting behind a camera by myself in my house. My wife is off in the distance and I'm preaching to our congregation without the band, without the choir and especially without the fellowship, the hugs, the kisses and the touch. No one can imagine what a pastor went through during that time unless you were a pastor. It felt like a part of you was not only snatched away, but you started to feel empty. I've had many friends and coworkers in the ministry as well as pastors and bishops who were dying all across this nation. Churches where I had frequently preached and held concerts would get the news that the pastor died. I was invited to go to one of the funerals but, for some reason, I couldn't make it. We later discovered after the funeral many bishops and pastors died. I'm pretty sure it was because of how funerals were orchestrated. Many were asked to give two minutes for expression and apparently, they were all using the same mic. God spared my life because I couldn't get to that funeral, yet I had no idea what was waiting for me. I did a concert in San Diego, CA on the USS Midway aircraft carrier on the flight deck. There was a large crowd and it was one of those kind of concerts where everything went right. We had such a powerful time. It was a great experience, but when I got back home the next day, late that evening, I got really sick. I was coughing really badly and throwing up. All of a sudden, I could barely breathe. So, my wife put me in the car and drove us to Philadelphia from Dover, DE, about an hour and twenty minutes away. We didn't know what was wrong but, of course, in the back of our minds we were both thinking COVID. When we arrived at the hospital, we pulled up to the emergency area where a security guard told us he was sorry, but we could not come inside. The hospital was filled to capacity, and he was trying to give us directions to another hospital in Philadelphia. I don't know what happened but, all of a sudden, he changed his mind and said, *"Well, come on."* I was placed in a wheelchair and rolled into the emergency area while my wife parked the car. I sat there for a moment or two and looked around seeing dozens and dozens of people affected by COVID. I remember them checking my oxygen level at the point of me almost fainting. I had such a high fever and, when they noticed my oxygen level, I was rushed in front of all those people who had been sitting there waiting. They rushed me into the emergency area and that's all I remember. I passed out and when I woke up, I was in intensive care. I had a ventilator in my throat and was told I had contracted COVID. It was a perfect storm because of my kidney transplant and the medicines I took, so my body wouldn't fight the kidney and see it as a foreign object. It also affected my immune system. COVID oppressed it and so having that virus was a perfect storm waiting to happen. I was in intensive care where they almost lost me. I was so afraid, but I was trying to pray and trust God at the same time. So many people around me were dying. I had to deal with the mental factor that bishops and pastors were dying from churches where I had preached and done concerts. I was asking myself, *"Is it my turn? Will I die? Oh God, oh God, oh God!"* We began to run tests because it was affecting other parts of my body. It was affecting my heart and my kidneys and got really bad. Not to mention, no one could come to see me because it was COVID! After several weeks, things started getting better, and it appeared I had survived the worst of it. I was still in intensive care, but things were much better. I asked the nurse, because it had been about a month now, could they at least roll me in the chair around the hallway, and they did. Now, what I didn't know is the only way out of that hospital, was to be released from intensive care. You don't go home from intensive care. You have to go to another floor and get much better first. One day, one of my mentors, a spiritual father, Bishop Thomas Weeks, Sr., heard I was in the hospital. He came to visit. When he came in my room, he patted me on my head, pulled up a chair and sat there praising God and speaking in tongues for about an hour. When he finished, we didn't have any conversation. He basically just patted me on my head and before leaving he said, *"You're going to be all right son."* After he left, from that point on, every test they took came back negative and I started getting better. After another week or so, I heard the hospital staff say, *"You're going down to the 4th floor."* Oh, I'll never forget that! I remember the day they rolled me out of intensive care. I said to one of my spiritual daughters named, Nelly, who visited me every day, *"Turn around and take a picture of this room because I want to remember where God had brought me from."* They took me down to the 4th floor, which was really different because you were more independent there. Many things they did in intensive care you had to do for yourself. I think I stayed on the 4th floor for another week before they began preparing me for discharge. That day my spiritual daughter rolled me out of the hospital while my wife got the car. In the car I had an oxygen tank as well, and my wife drove me home. Interestingly, when we got to Dover, she said she needed to run by the church first if it was okay with me. I was thinking, shouldn't I be going home? I had a walker as well. She got me to the church; my wife is so full of surprises. When I got out of the car, many of the members were standing outside and inside with balloons and cards. They were just celebrating the fact that God allowed me to come home. I went inside with my walker. I sat there and had remarks. I thanked them for their prayers and thanked God for my wife and our church. I went home with my oxygen tank, and it was good to be home. About two days later, I was sitting and watching TV, before my wife and I went to bed, and noticed I wasn't feeling as good as I was when I first came home. We went to bed, and I still had oxygen under my nose, but I couldn't sleep. We checked my oxygen levels, which started dropping and I got nervous. The level had dropped down to the 40s and got so bad I could barely breathe. My wife went into the kitchen and phoned the doctors and, eventually, had to call 911. When the paramedics got there, I was still conscious. They were asking questions, and I was answering them. They couldn't believe my oxygen level was so low. I was able to talk to them. When they put that oxygen cup over my nose and my mouth, it felt so good. The simple things we take for granted, just to be able to breathe! They rolled me out of the house, put me in the back of the ambulance and were prepared to drive me to the hospital in Dover. That's all I remember because I blanked out. When we arrived at the hospital, I eventually woke up and felt much better. They discovered I still had pneumonia behind my lungs, not COVID. I was suffering from the effects of the disease. It was affecting my breathing, heart, kidneys and things got worse. My wife left and when she came back, she was confused about what happened because I was intubated. I don't remember any of that. I was intubated and things got worse. They called my wife one day and said, *"We don't think he is going to survive,"* and to call the family together. My wife wouldn't accept that and called several people, she knew who could pray and would pray. She called the University of Penn because the Holy Spirit told her to get me out of that hospital. They had no beds available, but she prayed anyway. Eventually, they called my wife and said, *"We have a bed."* So, they flew me back by helicopter to the University of Penn. I don't even remember the ride because I was still intubated. When I got there, they began to work on me. I couldn't understand why the hospital in Delaware did some of the things they did, as I still had COVID. I remember being admitted to the medical center at the University of Penn. In intensive care again! This was the second time in one month that I'm back in the hospital. Things got bad again. Things were so bad they called my wife and said they didn't know if I was going to make it through the night. But the Saints of God were praying all across the country, even in Europe. I had people praying in Paris, France and in many parts of the world. I survived that night, but noticed there was a tube in my throat so I couldn't talk. Several weeks would go by and I didn't hear my voice. God began to turn things around. I started getting better. I was in the hospital for three and a half months. When it was time for me to leave the hospital, I remember them saying, *"You've got to go to physical therapy."* So, they put me in the back of the ambulance and drove me two hours to Milford, Delaware, where I would have to learn how to walk all over again. This was a challenging time because I'd been away from home so long. I missed my birthday, my wedding anniversary, Thanksgiving and was trying to get home for Christmas. God made it happen! On December 20th I went home, this time with no oxygen. I was thinking, one day while I was at home, about how the enemy tried to kill me one night as I was laying there and fell asleep. At one or two in the morning, I woke up because I couldn't breathe. I was the only one in my room and the nursing station was way down the hall. Something was stuck in my throat. The remote to call them was on the floor and I couldn't reach it. I couldn't get out of bed and so I panicked. I mean I panicked! Oh, my God, I panicked because I thought this was it! God, please! I had no way of contacting the nurses and, on top of that, just a few days before I was talking to one of my sisters and saying to them, *"I know you guys can't come see me but, my wife, she can't just give you a report every day. So, I need you guys to back off and she'll contact you."* She got upset and said, *"You're telling me we're down here praying for you and you're gonna talk to me like that?"* First of all, I had a trach in my throat so there was no way I could raise my voice. I told my sister, *"I just need you guys to back off of my wife and give her some space because she has a lot of responsibility. She's dealing with me, she's dealing with the record company, she's dealing with the church, she's dealing with all the other businesses that we have."* My sister said, *"I hope you die in intensive care,"* and hung up the phone. So now it's the middle of the night, and I'm panicking because I can't breathe thinking this is it. I can't call the nurses; I'm reaching for the remote and can't get it. The words that my sister said are rehearsing through my mind, *"I hope you die in intensive care."* I'm continuing to think this is it and start panicking again and calling God, *"Oh God, help me, Lord God, please, Lord God, don't let this be it."* I'm thinking this in my mind because I can't really talk, and I started breathing really hard. I mean breathing hard when, all of a sudden, the Holy Spirit said to me, *"Peace to you."* Yes, He did! I heard it. He said, *"Peace to you."* Then He said, *"Breathe, just take it easy and breathe."* So, I laid back and I just tried my best to breathe, even though it was still hard, but I wanted to obey the Holy Ghost. All of a sudden, he whispered something to me I didn't even know was possible. The Holy Spirit said, *"Disconnect the trach from the front of the tube,"* and when I did, that whistle blew, and the room went off. The nurses came running five deep. I pointed toward my trach, and they lifted it up and put this thing in my throat. I don't know what you call it, but it cleaned out my trach. I wish I knew the name of that piece of equipment. It's kind of like what the dentist uses when you know they want to remove the saliva out of your mouth. While they were working and I couldn't breathe, the power of God was with me. The enemy tried to kill me, but God wouldn't let it happen. Now, it's been three years and there are no complications and no trouble. The Lord said to me after we got out of the hospital, *"I can trust you now."* I'm like, wow, because my faith never wavered. I don't believe He said, *"I can trust you now"* because He didn't think He could. I think He said that more for me than Himself. That I could be trusted. That's when God began to speak to my wife and I, that He would relocate us back out to California. He said, *"I've used twenty-two years in the East to prepare you for the West. I'm going to use you to gather the Saints that's been scattered."*

God gave me my sight back when I was blind. When I had a heart attack 1,000 miles away from home, God let me survive. When I died after the surgery with the transplant, God brought me back to life. When I contracted COVID and almost died twice after three and a half months, God let me come out of the hospital and today I'm pastoring a church here in Los Angeles, Frontline Ministries. I'm traveling more now than I ever have in my career. God is allowing the music to bless people across the country and around the world. I feel better now than I ever have, and I give God glory. May I encourage you, that no matter what you face, no matter what you go through, your first priority is to trust God. What I have learned through all of this is that God has allowed me to survive and that his silence was not His absence. He was always there.

You Haven't Heard His Voice, But You See His Hand

Once, while I was in intensive care after about two months, I thought about it. I said, *"God, I haven't heard your voice."* In other words, I haven't heard the Holy Spirit speak to me. When I said that He said, *"No, you haven't heard His voice, but you've seen His hand."* My God! You've seen His hand! So, God's silence is not His absence. He's always there for you. I pray you are encouraged by these testimonies. I know there are other challenges I will face in my future, but I would always look back over my shoulder and say to myself, if He did it once, He can do it again.

In this book, I have shared with you my journey of faith and my journey of forgiveness. I've also talked about the pain of my past. How life has evolved because I was able to make decisions that propelled me into my destiny. How I did it…I held on to God. I put God first and, no matter what I faced, I placed my trust in His Word. The old Saints used to say,

"He may not come when you want Him but He's always on time." The Bible says, *"Being confident of this one thing, He which hath begun a good work in you will perform it until the day of the Lord Jesus Christ."*

It was 2018, and I don't think anything could have prepared me for this major trial I would face. When I was blind, I could still smile and enjoy people until God brought my sight back. I used to say when preaching blind, *"Hang in there!"* People were getting saved, joining the church, and I would tell them, *"Hang in there! Keep coming! I will see you again!"* That's what happened when I had a heart attack in my recovery. I was surrounded by people who made me laugh, prayed with me and helped usher me back to health. When my wife gave me her kidney, even after the transplant, even after I experienced death, I was surrounded by people who loved me, kept me encouraged, prayed for me and helped me back to health, even through COVID! Now, that was major because of the isolation for three and a half months in the hospital. Even when my wife eventually came and visited, I almost didn't recognize her because she had to put on a lot of hospital gear. When I was finally released, she drove me to the church where there was a large celebration with balloons, cards and well-wishes from the congregation. But nothing could prepare me for the darkest season I've ever experienced in my life. I woke up one morning feeling down and couldn't explain why. I would go to church and preach and the whole time I was preaching I was thinking I can't wait until I'm finished so I can go home. I began to isolate myself and didn't understand why. My wife recommended, and even my doctor recommended, I go talk to a therapist. In talking to the therapist, we discovered I had acute depression because of so many things hitting me at one time. I didn't know how to deal with it and fell into a dark place. That's the only way I can describe it. Now that I look back, it was a combination of things. Friends who turned their back on me because they were jealous of my success, family members who turned away from me because I refused to help them continuously, and the church I was pastoring had accumulated a large piece of property. It was a major 30,000 square feet shopping center. We had developed our sanctuary, administrative office, school of ministry, bookstore, and even our crystal room, which was like a dining area that seated about 500 people. The truth is the church really couldn't afford it from the beginning. I would take my royalties and monies I made on the road with my concerts and invest in it. I always believed that if I built it, if I helped get it done, they would pay for it. But eventually and, for no reason, even to this day I don't understand why people started leaving the church. It is amazing as a pastor when you have invested time into the lives of people, developing and discipling them, preaching at their family funerals, doing their baby dedications, performing their weddings, counseling sessions between the families, children, husbands and wives, and they leave. I think sometimes the congregation does not understand how much the pastor really loves them and considers them as sheep. With people leaving without me knowing, it took its toll and affected us financially. Our goal was to purchase the shopping center, but I ran into a brick wall. I knew if we didn't raise the money, in a certain number of years, the lease purchase to buy would be too expensive for us. Still, I was confident we could do it. When we were just about prepared to enter into a mortgage with the complex, we discovered from the owner that the property was in a bundled loan with several other pieces of property he owned. He really didn't know; he wasn't cheating us. I know this to be fact. We discovered from the banks that they would not allow him to take that one piece of property out of the bundle loan and sell it to us unless that whole loan was paid off. He didn't have the money to pay off the bundle loan. So, here we are now in a major shopping center and the only way out is to raise the total, which was five million dollars. This was difficult to do because, by that time, the monthly lease payment was astronomical. Not to mention payroll, electricity, insurance, and all the other things that go with running a ministry. It was difficult to save the money. I think, too, because we were at it so long, many of the people became discouraged and started leaving. That's when it hit me. I remember the first day we had to make a decision to let one of the units go. It was our bookstore. We had the best bookstore in the whole city. People were coming from other churches and throughout the city, but we couldn't afford it any longer. We liquidated all of the products in the bookstore and, not long after that, we had to let the school of ministry go. That's where I taught "Back to the Bible" for over eleven years, eleven graduations, eleven semesters, and, now, we had to let it go. In the process, a restaurant, which was more like a bar restaurant, moved into those two buildings. So, now we have our church in the same shopping center with a bar where people would come late at night, and even on weekends and sometimes in the day, drinking, playing music and partying. And, we're in this shopping center as well.

Then, all of a sudden, the finances dropped so low I had to let go of the Crystal Room. That was special to me. We have spent hundreds and thousands of dollars in renovating it. I spent thousands and thousands of my personal money thinking if we got it built, the Saints would rent it. We could do parties, banquets and events for the city, which would pay for itself, and eventually begin to turn a profit. It could even become a part of helping to pay off the shopping center's beautiful crystal room. I kind of molded my church after my home church, West Angeles Church of God in Christ. Bishop Charles Blake was my spiritual father and mentor, but I had to let it go.

My Greatest Challenge, Depression

At the same time, my wife and I were in the process of adopting a child, a little boy who was six years old. My wife and I didn't have any children together. She has a son named Shelton and I have two sons and a daughter. In the process of adopting him, it didn't work out. There were some issues. He was having major mental challenges, but he was in my heart. I made a promise to him I would never leave him. Like what happened to me when I was a small child. It hurt my heart that I could not adopt him. Between him, the church losing different people, my friends and my family, I fell to a dark place.

Depression is the mental pain that Tylenol cannot heal. I started staying in bed all day. My wife would get up and go to the office. I would be in the room in bed with the lights out and curtains pulled. I could just lay there all day with thoughts running through my mind a million miles a minute. I felt hopeless. It would be about 3:30 almost 4:00 in the afternoon and I'm still in bed. I began telling myself, *"Norman, get up. You've got to get up and go eat."*I wouldn't eat. I wasn't eating, I couldn't eat, and so I lost a lot of weight. I even changed Bible study because it was difficult for me to teach on Tuesday nights. God knows how difficult it was because I didn't want to hear the scriptures or anything about the scripture. It was hard for me to teach it because that's not where I was. I was living every day in a dark hole. Sometimes I would go to the mall and find a seat somewhere in a place where there was hardly any walking traffic. I could sit there and just think all day long. No one in the church knew what was going on with me because I knew how to fake it. I don't know if that's the best way to say it but that's what I was able to do. So, I stopped teaching Bible study on Tuesday nights and told the congregation we're just going to turn the night into a prayer night. We will come and pray for an hour. Every Tuesday while the congregation prayed, I would lay on the altar, and I would beg for help—that God would help me. I felt like I had on a winter coat that was oversized, and it was dark in color. I felt like there was a bag over my head and I could not breathe or see beyond the surface. I felt like at any moment something major was going to happen that would snatch the breath out of my body. I felt hopeless, I felt ashamed, I felt I had no one to understand. I'd lost so much! How can a man be so popular? People singing my music all across the nation and around the world, receiving Grammy Awards and gold and platinum albums and top charting songs, and yet I'm in a dark place. It is like walking through a graveyard in the dark.You didn't realize there was a hole there. You fell in it and no one came to help you out.

It got worse because my primary doctor recommended that I take medications. I guess that would kind of help suppress my feelings or whatever. I remember the first prescription. I took the pill but really didn't feel better, I just didn't think as much. I didn't think dark things because I got to a place where I could think about suicide all day and about one hundred different ways to take my life. The battle was within myself. Warning me to take my life, but trying to answer the question, "*Why should I take my life?*" at the same time. It was a battle all day that left me feeling like I had nothing to live for and like a failure. In my mind it felt like no one loved me, even though I was married and my wife loved me. She gave me space. There were so many things I was dealing with, and I didn't want to weigh her down. So, I didn't tell her. It had gotten to a point where I could be in bed, up until 3:30 in the morning. It's dark outside, my wife was at the office, and she called home to say, "*I'm just calling to check in and see how you are doing.*" I said, "*Well, I'm doing fine.*" She asked me, "*You're not still in bed, are you?*" I said, "*Oh, nooooo!I got up, took my shower and I'm out playing the piano and writing songs.*" That wasn't the truth. I had the cover pulled over my head, one minute praying for death, another minute praying for life. I was asking God to help me one minute, and the next minute I felt like I didn't deserve to live. This was a merry-go-round I wanted to get off. It was a mental pain I could not describe at that moment. I felt it would have been better for me to be blind than to deal with depression. At least when I was blind, I could smile, I could laugh. Even with any other sicknesses I had dealt with, I was still happy. I looked at myself in the mirror one morning while getting dressed and noticed I wasn't smiling. I also noticed that almost a year went by, and I had not smiled. As I looked in the mirror, I said to myself, *"You will smile again, you will laugh again, the joy soon will begin, and the pain soon will end."*Eventually, that would become a song titled, *Smiled Again.* In the meantime, I was in a dark depression. How I got through a sermon, only God knows. During that time, what I did was choose sermons that were easy to preach with no conviction. I didn't even believe it myself at the time. But, because I had been preaching for so long, I knew how to do it. People were still joining the church. They were laughing, they were happy. Out of the hundreds of people, I think the thing that puzzled me the most was not one person was spiritual enough to discern what their pastor was going through. I also felt as the leader, overseer and shepherd, I had to hide it from them. Pride had nothing to do with it. I was just afraid. I prayed for deliverance; I asked God to deliver me. It got to a point where I became addicted to the medications, so I went from bad to worse. I took the medication in the daytime, and it suppressed my feelings so I didn't think as much. Even though I didn't smile, I didn't really function to my maximum. I wasn't the happy Norman who loved to crack jokes, who loved to smile and loved to do pranks. I was able to function, I would say. Later in the afternoon, I could tell when the medication wore off because, all of a sudden, I'm thinking about suicide again. I'm thinking about hopelessness, that it's over for me and my future is dim. There was nothing positive in my thoughts. I'm just grateful I didn't speak it out of my mouth. The thoughts only existed in my mind. When I took the medication about an hour later, I still felt depressed. Felt better, just being depressed. That became the story of my life. Anytime I felt myself falling in that dark hole I took the medications, and they would allow me to function. If I got down to two or three pills left, I had to get the prescription renewed quickly because I didn't want to go a day without it. It got to a point where I was taking two a day now. I was addicted. I didn't know it at first, but I could tell I was. I prayed and asked God for deliverance. It's amazing to me because during that time I didn't hear His voice. The Holy Spirit really never talked to me. It's as if I was walking through that season by myself but, now, I do realize the Holy Spirit was talking. I just didn't want to hear Him. It wasn't helping me the way I wanted to be helped, but I kept calling on the name of the Lord. My wife kept praying for me. Sometimes, she would grab me and just hug me, and tears would fall from my face. I felt so bad because I felt like I wasn't the leader. I wasn't the strong tower, the strong man for my wife, leading her spiritually. I was in such a dark place.

Just Me and the Demons

My wife went on a trip to Los Angeles, and I stayed home. She was gone for three days, and I stayed in the house for three days. I did not leave, and I did not eat. It was like I was in a house with just me and demons. It was dark and cold. Sometimes it felt like I could hear voices, and then later it got worse. I had a gun in the house that I bought, but never shot it. It was kept there for protection just in case we needed it. I remember lying in bed. The gun was within reaching distance. I was thinking all night, one night to just end it all. I suffered through the night and thank God I never touched that gun. But, I sure thought about doing it. That means things were really bad. Things had gotten as bad as they could, and I really started crying out to God. He had His plan to deliver me, but the one thing I can say is even in the deepest, darkest bowels of my depression, I never cursed God. I never bad-mouthed God. Never! It's not that I didn't doubt God, it's that I didn't think God would help me. I thought maybe I'm paying a price for not being a good manager, or I don't know why I would be so successful and live my dream and feel no one loves me. Of course, I learned some major lessons behind this experience. Sometimes you're only valuable to people when you help them with your resources. I had a sibling ask me for $12,000 one-time and I said I can't do it. They said, "*Why not? You have it.*" I'm thinking to myself, *but I've been helping you with your mortgage and you can't pay that. How are you gonna pay me back $12,000?* It's been several years now since we've not spoken. I can go down the list of friends I've loaned money to who never paid me back, and it has affected our relationship. So, I'm asking God to deliver me, and He has an interesting way, sometimes, of answering your prayers.

My wife and I had to go to Los Angeles for about five days. We landed and checked into our hotel room. As I was unpacking my clothes, I realized I did not bring my medications. I started panicking because I was already feeling that darkness, that heavy coat starting to fall on me. Truth is, I was ready to fly all the way back 3,000 miles to Delaware to get my medication. I didn't know what to do. The later it got in the evening in Los Angeles, the worse I felt. I was having withdrawals, sweating, shaking and chills. My thoughts were telling me I was going to die. It was unbelievable. The later it got, the worse it got. My wife just prayed for me while I was in the bed, and I kept calling out the name of God, *"Help me, Lord! Help me, Lord!"* I eventually dozed off and fell asleep. When I woke up the next day, the depression was yet present, but it wasn't as bad. I was able to function enough to do what we had to do while we were there. Around 3:00 or 4:00 in the afternoon, I knew I needed that medication. I can't explain it. I just cannot explain it. I knew my body, my brain, and my mind needed it. I was dependent, addicted and here comes the chills again. Here comes the withdrawals again. I suffered, but I made it through the night and finally said to my wife, *"It's been two days with no medication."* We celebrated, but the night was coming. It always seemed as the sun was going down, depression hit the hardest. When you are depressed it's almost like you can think your way into dark place. You feel hopeless, unworthy, dried up and that God would not use you again. You know with all the loss I'd experienced, I think I put people in a place in my heart they shouldn't have been. So, when they walked away, I didn't know how to deal with the pain of rejection. I've been through it before when my father rejected and disowned me as his son. Now I have members of the church, friends and family treating me the same way. I just couldn't take it and felt death was a better option. But, I made it through the night. I started talking to my medication and my depression saying, *"I beat you three nights and if I can do three, I can do four!"* I made it through the fourth night, and I began feeling much better than the first, second and even the third night. I couldn't believe it. I started eating, I had lost so much weight, I almost didn't recognize myself in the mirror. But the fifth day, I'm telling you, I almost felt like myself again. My wife and I had fun that day and she was so happy. Just to see her smile, even though I didn't smile. She would try to tickle me to make me laugh or do something crazy and just act silly. I just looked at her. God, I thank you for my wife who stuck by me through all that I've been through.

We're on the plane flying back home now. We walked into the house. When I walked in my bedroom, the first thing that caught my attention was my medication sitting on the dresser. I walked up to it, looked at it and said to it, *"I beat you five days, and if I can do five, I can do six!"* I refused to move it and left it right there on the counter! I'll beat it on the sixth day! The thoughts of suicide went away, and the thoughts of hopelessness started leaving because my wife started speaking life to me, saying, *"God is not finished with you yet, stop blaming yourself for everybody else's mistakes, you're not their God, you're not Superman, you're Norman! We make bad choices and decisions, but that doesn't have to be our life story!"* The seventh day, I looked at the medications and said, *"I beat you six day.s I'm going to beat you seven!"* and I did! I never moved the medication from the dresser. When I got to about ten days of talking to that medication, I could tell the depression was gone. I brushed my teeth and after I cleaned my mouth, I thought about something that made me smile. Wow! God, I give you praise! I looked in the mirror. I was smiling at myself and started talking to myself in the mirror. I said, *"Norman I'm proud of you. You're going to be okay; you're going to be okay."* Every day got better and better, like someone who injured their foot and had to walk on crutches for a season. Then, eventually, the foot healed and they put the crutches down. That's what the medication was for me.

I remember the Sunday I stood up at church and gave my testimony about going through depression, and no one had a clue. It was so quiet you could hear a pin drop. I preached and ministered. I could tell I was delivered because I felt the anointing of God, the power of God, and I was walking in victory. The church was packed that Sunday, I will never forget it. When I finished preaching, the Holy Spirit led me to do an altar call. When I said, *"There may be some of you in here today like me. Privately you are dealing with depression and anxiety. I want to pray for you because the same God that brought me through and delivered me, He's here for you today."* I had no idea that because of what I experienced and went through, almost a year of depression, would bring healing and deliverance to so many. People started coming to the altar from every corner of the sanctuary and, eventually, the altar was full. You almost couldn't get another person at the altar. I just stood there thinking to myself, *"My God, this many people? Maybe one or two, but the altar is full of people dealing with anxiety and depression. It was worth it all for me to have gone through what I went through, if it was meant to bring healing and deliverance to so many."*

We prayed that day and, I'm telling you, the power of God fell in that place. It almost sounded like a funeral because people were wailing and mourning. I mean, you could hear the deep dark cry that was familiar to me. I went through the same thing. Many of them were delivered from their depression and their anxiety. When I left church that day, I was praising and thanking God, *"Now, I understand why you allow us to go through certain things."* The Bible says, *"For we have not a high priest who cannot be touched with the feeling of our infirmities, but he was tempted in all points like as we are yet without sin."* Sometimes, going through challenges, circumstances, and situations is a part of your spiritual growth. God is building your testimony so when you walk in victory, you can snatch someone else out of their dark place. David said, *"It was good for me to have been afflicted."* It doesn't feel like it in the midst of it, but when you experience victory, God wants to use your testimony. He will use your deliverance to bring healing and deliverance to other people. So, I pray for all of you today who were led by the Spirit of God to read Chapter 12. Those who have been or who may be going through what God brought me out of. I just want to tell you, today is the beginning of your deliverance and your victory because whom the Son has set free he is free indeed.

A Winner Never Quits, A Quitter Never Wins

The greatest gift God has ever given to men is the gift of life. And, the second greatest gift God has given to men is self-will. The ability to choose and make choices and decisions. To become whatever you desire, and no matter what life brings your way, you fight to overcome it. A winner never quits, and a quitter never wins. As I look back over my life at all the things I've gone through physically and mentally, God was there all the time. Making the right choices and right decisions by using the wisdom of God's Word is essential to your victory.

I will close with this. There was a farmer who had a dying horse, and he wanted to sell it before it died. There was a city man just cruising through the countryside when he saw the for-sale sign. He always wanted a horse. So, he stopped and asked the farmer how much the horse was. The farmer said $200. The city man, who was also an accountant, said that sounds to be very cheap for a beautiful horse like that. He asked, *"Why is he so cheap?"* The farmer lied and said, *"He used to run in the Kentucky Derby and now he's retired. We just have him here to live out the rest of his life, but I'd rather sell him to someone who will enjoy him and love him. You can't ride him really fast, but you can ride him around your pasture."* The city man was so excited. So, he bought the horse and paid $200. He said to the farmer, *"I'll be back next week to pick him up."* So, he left and, while he was away, the horse died. When the city man came back to pick up the horse, he brought a trailer with him to load him up. The farmer said, *"I'm sorry the horse died."* The city man was so disappointed because he had already made arrangements for the horse. He had a place to keep him, and he was even going to rename him. So, finally, the city man says to the farmer. *"Well, do I get a refund?"* The farmer said, *"No, all sales are final." "But, the horse is dead!"* said the city man. *"Yeah, but when you bought him, he was alive,"* said the farmer. The city man, the accountant thought about it. Then he says, *"Okay, well, help me load him up on my truck."* The farmer asked, *"What are you gonna do with a dead horse?"* and the city man responded, *"I'm going to sell him."* The farmer asks, *"What do you mean? You're gonna sell a dead horse? Who's gonna buy a dead horse?"* The city man didn't say anything else and left with the dead horse. Being an accountant he had a great idea. He made 200 raffle tickets. He sold each one for $50 and raffled off the dead horse. One day he was back out on the countryside and ran into the farmer. The farmer said, *"Hey, city man, what did you do with the dead horse?"* He said, *"I sold him."* The farmer said, *"Are you telling me someone bought a dead horse?"* He said, *"Yes."* The farmer asked him, *"How did you do that?"* The city man said, *"Well I made-up 200 tickets, I sold them for $50 each and I made $10,000."* The farmer said, *"So, somebody won the horse?"* He said, *"Yes, somebody won the horse."* The farmer asked, *"Well, what did he do when he found out the horse was dead?"* The city man said, *"I refunded him his $50."* So, the city man made $9,750 from a dead horse.

The moral of the story is you have a choice. You can either complain about it or do something about it. No matter what hand life deals you, win with it! Win with it, no matter what tragic circumstances or situations you may have to go through. Win with it, because greater is He that is in you than he that is in the world.

I pray you've been blessed, inspired and encouraged with the words of this book. May the grace of our Lord and Savior Jesus Christ be with you forever. Amen.

Mrs. Karen Hutchins & Dr. Norman E. Hutchins

REFERENCES

The Holy Bible, King James Version, Public Domain.

Ebony Magazine, Founder John H. Johnson, Johnson Publishing Company, 1945-2016. (Source: en.m.wikipedia.org).

JDI Records, Founder James Roberson, 1998. (Source: journalofgospel music.com).

YouTube [Social Media], Founders Steve Chen, Chad Hurley, and Jawed Karim, Owned by Google LLC, 2005. (Source: en.m.wikipedia.org).

Sparrow Records, Founder Billy Ray Hearn, 1976. (Source: en.m.wikipedia.org).

Capitol Records, Founders Johnny Mercer, Buddy DeSylva, Glenn Wallichs, 1942. (Source: en.m.wikipedia.org).

Are We Really Doing Your Will? [Song], *Introducing The Winans* Album, performed by The Winans, Yell Records, 1995. (Source: open.spotify.com).

Good Times [TV Show], created by Mike Evans, Norman Lear, Eric Monte, Tandem Productions, 1974-1979. (Source: www.imdb.com).

Bee Movie [Film], written by Jerry Seinfeld, Spike Feresten, Barry Marder, Andy Robin, Additional Screenplay Material by Chuck Martin, Tom Papa, Dreamworks Animation, Columbus 81 Productions, 2007. (Source: www.imdb.com).

The Andy Griffith Show [TV Show], created by Sheldon Leonard, Aaron Ruben, Danny Thomas, CBS, Danny Thomas Enterprises, Mayberry Enterprises, Paramount Television, 1960-1968. (Source: www.imdb.com).

Bayside Gospel Concert Aboard the Midway, performance by Norman Hutchins, USS Midway Museum, San Diego, California, produced by M.A.N.D.A.T.E. Records, 2021. (Source: M.A.N.D.A.T.E. Records).

For Speaking Engagements, Book Signings, Appearances, and Interviews,

Contact:
Karen Hutchins

Phone:
(302) 399-5169

Email:
karenhutchins@irmusicgroup.com

Address:
6709 La Tijera, #441
Los Angeles, CA 90045

Website:
www.irmusicgroup.com

Facebook / Instagram / Twitter:
IR Music Group
Norman Hutchins

Made in the USA
Columbia, SC
22 April 2025